A GUIDE TO EXPOSITORY MINISTRY

A Guide to Expository Ministry:
Guide Book No. 003
Copyright © 2012 by SBTS Press.

SBTS Press c/o Communications
2825 Lexington Ave.
Louisville, KY 40280

Printed in the United States of America.

ISBN: 978-0615706832

A GUIDE TO

Expository Ministry

Dan Dumas, Editor

GUIDE BOOK NO. *003*

———

To the army of faithful expositors who
explicate God's Word around the globe

– *Dan Dumas*

———

TABLE OF CONTENTS

—

INTRODUCTION

—

EXPOSITORY MINISTRY

A Comprehensive Vision

Dan Dumas

When God speaks, creation obeys. When he spoke the universe into existence, it happened (Gen 1:3-26). When he speaks into the cold, dead hearts of sinners, a new creation appears (2 Cor 5:17). When preachers exposit the Word of God and announce that Jesus is the Christ, the church is built (Matt 16:16-18). Whenever God's Word is proclaimed, something comes into existence that wasn't there before.

Even a casual observation of the evangelical landscape reveals that much of this church-building, Christ-centered, truth-driven, gospel-proclaiming, expository preaching has turned into, well, something else. If the church is going to flourish, then something needs to change.

The Preaching

If you're reading this book, it's likely that you're familiar with expository preaching. Maybe you've heard it before, maybe you hear it every week or maybe you do it every week at your church. Expository preaching happens when a preacher lays open a biblical text so that its original meaning is brought to bear on the lives of contemporary listeners. Expository preaching is a call to deliver from the pulpit what has already been delivered in the Scriptures. If this happens at your church every week, then praise God. This is the kind of preaching God's people have always needed – and nothing has changed. It's the kind of preaching that Christ modeled when he explained to his disciples

> Faithful, expository preaching is being replaced with whatever scratches the itching ears of our self-centered, consumerist culture.

"the things concerning himself in all the Scriptures" (Lk 24:27). It's the kind of preaching commanded in the Great Commission, practiced in the early church, reinforced in Paul's Pastoral Epistles and demonstrated throughout church history. It's not the job of the preacher to improve upon the program God instituted in the first place.

Unfortunately, many churches aren't getting expository preaching from the pulpit. This is a primary cause for the epidemic of biblical illiteracy in the pews. Preachers aren't teaching the Bible, and they're not teaching their people how to read it and study it for themselves. Not surprisingly, people grow disinterested in the Bible.

Faithful, expository preaching is instead being replaced with whatever scratches the itching ears of our self-centered, consumerist culture. Ironically, this pursuit of relevance has achieved just the opposite. People don't see the immediate impact that the Bible has on their lives because preachers are too busy trying to chase the bankrupt idol that is relevance.

Why has expository preaching been exchanged for this pragmatism? Because it's hard work. It takes serious commitment

> If God's people are going to be presented "mature in Christ," then biblical, expository preaching needs to return to the sacred desk of local churches.

to spend time studying week-in and week-out, praying through the text, allowing it to marinate the preacher's own soul, spending time in the original languages, trying to place himself in the first century and reading the insights of men past and present with more wisdom than he.

If God's people are going to be presented "mature in Christ" (Col 1:28), then biblical, expository preaching needs to return to the sacred desk of local churches. If you're working faithfully to exposit the Scriptures, then this book will encourage you to excel still more and give you some allies along the way. If you're wondering if the Bible is what your people really need, then this book will call you back and remind you that God provides all his people need in his Word (2 Tim 3:16). All he calls preachers to do is open the Bible, study it and proclaim its message.

The Preacher

Expository preaching, however, is about more than preaching. It's about preaching and the preacher; the ministry and the man. People need preaching grounded in and guided by the Scriptures, and they need preachers grounded in and guided by the Scriptures.

There's a reason the majority of the biblical qualifications for leadership in the local church center on character (1 Tim 3:1-13; Titus 1:6-9). Such a noble calling requires noble character. The last thing the church needs is a preacher who preaches against adultery one day, and is found guilty of it the next, or a preacher who preaches self-control, but clearly lacks it in the way he uses the Web, consumes and eats. Churchgoers know they can trust the preaching in their pulpit only as far as they can trust the preacher who steps into it every week. The fruitfulness of a man's ministry will never exceed that of his life.

God's people need expository preaching from godly men who lead expository lives and do expository ministry. If the man is going to be an expositor in the pulpit, then he had better be an expositor in the study, in the home, in the prayer meeting, at the kids' soccer games and all the other places where he lives out God's call on his life (i.e., everywhere). The same commitment demanded in the study lays claim on the entirety of the preacher's life and is to be applied relentlessly, the commitment to live out God's Word as the final authority rather than our own minds. A commitment to this kind of lifestyle is the recipe for faithful, expository preaching and faithful, expository ministry.

And a funny thing happens when preachers start living faithfully and start preaching the Bible: their people start to want more of it. Your church members will begin to recognize that God's Word is to

> The fruitfulness of a man's ministry will never exceed that of his life.

be desired more than gold, and is sweeter than the honeycomb (Ps 19:10). They start to crave the "solid food" of God's Word (Heb 5:12). They can't get enough of it. They want to hear more preaching and teaching. They want to know how to get more out of the sermon. They become grateful for faithful preaching. They want to know how to read and study the Bible for themselves. They want to know what resources they can take advantage of in their personal study.

And if you're a preacher, you want this for your people, but you must remember that your church will never esteem God's Word any higher than you do.

The People

But we're not just equipping and encouraging preachers here. We're going beyond the preaching, past the preacher to his people, the recipients of the expositor's ministry. The goal is never to have one guy in the church (the preacher) who knows how to read his Bible and how to use it to have an impact on people's lives. Local churches should brim with people equipped to use their Bibles in their own lives and that of those around them.

When Luther and the Reformers advocated for the priesthood of all believers, they were reminding

Local churches should brim with people equipped to use their Bibles.

Christians that individual people are ultimately responsible for the eternal state of their soul.

So, whether you're in a church with consistently edifying sermons or with crummy, boring preaching, you are the one who will stand before God. So it's important for you to know how to grow in the grace and knowledge of Christ (2 Pet 3:18). Fortunately, God has not left us alone in this glorious task. He has given us fellow believers, the local church, pastors, the canon of Scripture and the Holy Spirit. Indeed, he has "granted to us all things that pertain to life and godliness" (2 Pet 1:3).

If you're someone who wants to learn how to get the most out of the revelation God has given – by improving your ability to listen to sermons, read the Bible and be a more faithful church member – then this book is for you: expository preaching from an expository preacher for an expository people. ◉

A GUIDE TO EXPOSITORY MINISTRY

—

FOR THE PREACHER

—

THE CENTER OF WORSHIP

Expository Preaching

R. Albert Mohler Jr.

Evangelical Christians have been especially attentive to worship in recent years, sparking a renaissance of thought and conversation concerning what worship really is and how it should be done. Even if this renewed interest has unfortunately resulted in what some have called the "worship wars" in some churches, it seems that what A.W. Tozer once called the "missing jewel" of evangelical worship is being recovered.

Entertainment, Evangelism or Exposition?

Nevertheless, if most evangelicals would quickly agree that worship is central to the life of the church, there would be no consensus to an unavoidable question: "What is central to Christian worship?" Historically, the more liturgical churches argued that the sacraments form the heart of Christian worship. These churches argue that the elements of the Lord's Supper and the water of baptism most powerfully present the gospel. Among evangelicals, some present a call for evangelism as the heart of worship, planning every facet of the service – songs, prayers, sermons – with the evangelistic invitation in mind.

Though most evangelicals mention the preaching of the Word as a necessary or customary part of worship, the prevailing model of worship in evangelical churches is increasingly defined by music, along with innovations such as drama and video presentations. When preaching retreats, a host of entertaining innovations will take its place.

Traditional norms of worship are now subordinated to a demand for relevance and creativity. A media-driven culture of images has replaced the word-centered culture that gave birth to the Reformation churches. In some sense, the image-driven culture of modern evangelicalism is an embrace of the very practices rejected by the Reformers in their quest for true biblical worship.

Music fills the space in most evangelical worship, and much of this music comes in the form of contemporary choruses marked by precious little theological content. Beyond the popularity of the chorus as a musical form, many evangelical churches seem intensely concerned to replicate studio-quality musical presentations.

In terms of musical style, the more traditional churches feature large choirs – often with orchestras – and may even sing the established hymns of the faith. Choral contributions are often massive in scale and professional in quality. In any event, music fills the space and drives the energy

When preaching retreats, a host of entertaining innovations will take its place.

of the worship service. Intense planning, financial investment and preparation are invested in the musical dimensions of worship. Professional staff and an army of volunteers spend much of the week in rehearsals and practice sessions.

All of this investment in the musical dimension of worship is not lost on the congregation. Some Christians shop congregations in order to find the church that offers the worship style and experience that fits their expectation. In most communities, churches are known for their worship styles and musical programs. Those dissatisfied with what they find at one church can quickly move to another, sometimes using the language of self-expression to explain that the new church "meets our needs" or "allows us to worship."

A concern for true biblical

The heart of Christian worship is the authentic preaching of the Word of God.

worship was at the very heart of the Reformation. But even Martin Luther, who wrote hymns and required his preachers to be trained in song, would not recognize this modern preoccupation with music as legitimate or healthy. Why? Because the Reformers were convinced that the heart of true biblical worship was the preaching of the Word of God.

Thanks be to God, evangelism does take place in Christian worship. Confronted by the presentation of the gospel and the preaching of the Word, sinners are drawn to faith in Jesus Christ and the offer of salvation is presented to all who so respond. Likewise, the Lord's Supper and baptism are honored as ordinances by the Lord's own command, and each finds its place in true worship.

Furthermore, music is one of God's most precious gifts to his people, and it is a language by which we may worship God in spirit and in truth. The hymns of the faith convey rich confessional and theological content, and many modern choruses recover a sense of doxology formerly lost in many evangelical churches. But the central act of Christian worship is neither music, nor evangelism, nor even the ordinances. The heart of

Christian worship is the authentic preaching of the Word of God.

Preaching as Center

Expository preaching is central, irreducible and nonnegotiable to the Bible's mission of authentic worship that pleases God. John Stott's simple declaration states the issue boldly: "Preaching is indispensable to Christianity." More specifically, preaching is indispensable to Christian worship – and not only indispensable, but central.

The centrality of preaching is the theme of both testaments of Scripture. In Nehemiah 8 we find the people demanding that Ezra the scribe bring the book of the law to the assembly. Ezra and his colleagues stand on a raised platform and read from the book. When he opens the book to read, the assembly rises to its feet in honor of the Word of God and their response to the reading is to answer, "Amen, Amen!"

Interestingly, the text explains that Ezra and those assisting him "read from the book, from the Law of God, clearly, and they gave the sense, so that the people understood the reading" (Neh 8:8). This remarkable text presents a portrait of expository preaching. Once the text was read, it was carefully explained

In far too many churches, the Bible is nearly silent.

to the congregation. Ezra did not stage an event or orchestrate a spectacle – he simply and carefully proclaimed the Word of God.

This text is a sobering indictment of much contemporary Christianity. According to the text, a demand for biblical preaching erupted within the hearts of the people. They gathered as a congregation and summoned the preacher. This reflects an intense hunger and thirst for the preaching of the Word of God. Where is this desire evident among today's evangelicals?

In far too many churches, the Bible is nearly silent. The public reading of Scripture has been dropped from many services, and the sermon has been sidelined, reduced to a brief devotional appended to the music. Many preachers accept this as a necessary concession to the age of entertainment. Some hope to put in a brief message of encouragement or exhortation before the conclusion of the service.

As Michael Green so pointedly

put it: "This is the age of the sermonette, and sermonettes make Christianettes."

The anemia of evangelical worship – all the music and energy aside – is directly attributable to the absence of genuine expository preaching. Such preaching would confront the congregation with nothing less than the living and active Word of God. That confrontation will shape the congregation as the Holy Spirit accompanies the Word, opens eyes and applies that Word to human hearts.

Expository Preaching

If preaching is central to Christian worship and the remedy that evangelical worship needs, what kind of preaching are we talking about? The sheer weightlessness of much contemporary preaching is a severe indictment of our superficial Christianity. When the pulpit ministry lacks substance, the church is severed from the Word of God, and its health and faithfulness are immediately diminished.

Many evangelicals are seduced by the proponents of topical and narrative preaching. The declarative force of Scripture is blunted by a demand for story, and the textual shape of the Bible is supplanted by topical considerations. In many pul-

> When the pulpit ministry lacks substance, the church is severed from the Word of God, and its health and faithfulness are immediately diminished.

pits, the Bible, if referenced at all, becomes merely a source for pithy aphorisms or convenient narratives.

The therapeutic concerns of the culture too often set the agenda for evangelical preaching. Issues of the self predominate, and the congregation expects to hear simple answers to complex problems. Furthermore, postmodernism claims intellectual primacy in the culture, and even if they do not surrender entirely to doctrinal relativism, the average congregant expects to make his or her own final decisions about all important issues of life, from worldview to lifestyle.

Authentic Christian preaching carries a note of authority and a demand for decisions not found elsewhere in society. The solid truth of Christianity stands in stark contrast to the flimsy pretensions of postmodernity. Unfortunately, the appetite for serious preaching has virtually disappeared among many Christians, who are content to have their fascinations with themselves encouraged from the pulpit.

One of the first steps to a recovery of authentic Christian preaching is to define exactly what we mean when we discuss authentic preaching as exposition. Many preachers claim to be expositors, but in many cases this means no more than that the preacher has a biblical text in mind, no matter how tenuous may be the actual relationship between the text and the sermon.

I offer the following definition of expository preaching as a framework for consideration:

"Expository preaching is that mode of Christian preaching that takes as its central purpose the presentation and application of the text of the Bible. All other issues and concerns are subordinated to the central task of presenting the biblical text. As the Word of God, the text of Scripture has the right to establish both the substance and the structure of the sermon. Genuine exposition takes place when the preacher sets forth the meaning and message of the biblical text and makes clear how the Word of God establishes the identity and worldview of the church as the people of God."

Expository preaching begins with the preacher's determination to present and explain the text of the Bible to his congregation. This simple starting point is a major issue of division in contemporary homiletics, for many preachers assume that they must begin with a human problem or question and then work backward to the biblical text. On the contrary, expository preaching begins with the text and works from the text to apply its truth to the lives of believers. If this determination and commitment are not clear at the outset, then something other than expository preaching will result.

The preacher always comes to the text and to the preaching event with many concerns and priorities in mind, many of which are undeniably legitimate and important in their own right. Nevertheless, if genuine exposition of the Word of God is to take place, those other concerns must be subordinate to the central and irreducible task of explaining and presenting the biblical text.

Expository preaching is inescapably bound to the serious work of exegesis. If the preacher is to explain the text, he must first study the text and devote the necessary hours of study and research necessary to understand the text. The pastor must invest the largest portion of his energy and intellectual engagement (not to mention his time) to this task of "rightly handling the word of truth" (2 Tim 2:15). There are no shortcuts to genuine exposition. The expositor is not an explorer who returns to tell tales of the journey, but a guide who leads the people into the text and teaches the arts of Bible study and interpretation even as he demonstrates the same.

Moreover, because the Bible is the inerrant and infallible Word of God, the shape of the biblical text is also therefore divinely directed. God has spoken through the inspired human authors of Scripture, and each different genre of biblical literature demands that the preacher give careful attention to the text, allowing it to shape the message. Far too many preachers come to the text with a sermonic shape in mind and a limited set of tools in hand. To be sure, the shape of the sermon may differ from preacher to preacher and should differ from text to text. But genuine exposition demands that the text establish the shape as well as the substance of the sermon.

The preacher rises in the pulpit to accomplish one central purpose – to set forth the message and meaning of the biblical text. This requires historical investigation, literary discernment and the faithful employment of the *analogia fidei* to interpret the Scripture by Scripture. It also requires the expositor to reject the modern conceit that what the text *meant* is not necessarily what it *means*. If the Bible is truly the enduring and eternal Word of God, it means what it meant as it is newly applied in every generation.

> The preacher rises in the pulpit to accomplish one central purpose – to set forth the message and meaning of the biblical text.

> Preaching is
> the essential
> instrumentality
> through which
> God shapes
> his people.

Once the meaning of the text is set forth, the preacher moves to application. Application of biblical truth is a necessary task of expository preaching. But application must follow the diligent and disciplined task of explaining the text itself. T.H.L. Parker describes preaching like this: "Expository preaching consists in the explanation and application of a passage of Scripture. Without explanation it is not expository; without application it is not preaching."

Application is absolutely necessary, but it is also fraught with danger. The first danger is the temptation to believe that the preacher can or should manipulate the human heart. The preacher is responsible for setting forth the eternal Word of Scripture. Only the Holy Spirit can apply that Word to human hearts or even open eyes to understand and receive the text.

Every sermon presents the hearer with a forced decision. We will either obey or disobey the Word of God. The sovereign authority of God operates through the preaching of his Word to demand obedience from his people. Preaching is the essential instrumentality through which God shapes his people as the Holy Spirit accompanies the preaching of the Word. As the Reformers remind us, it is through preaching that Christ is present among his people.

Defining the Solution: Authority, Reverence, Centrality

If expository preaching is at the center of worship, then what is it that comprises expository preaching? Authentic expository preaching is marked by three distinct characteristics: authority, reverence and centrality. Expository preaching is authoritative because it stands upon the very authority of the Bible as the Word of God. Such preaching requires and reinforces a sense of reverent expectation on the part of God's people. Finally, expository preaching demands the central place in Christian worship and is respected as the event through which the living God speaks to his people.

A keen analysis of our contemporary age comes from sociologist Richard Sennett of New York University. Sennett notes that in times past a major anxiety of most persons was loss of governing authority. Now, the tables have been turned, and modern persons are anxious about any authority over them: "We have come to fear the influence of authority as a threat to our liberties, in the family and in society at large." If previous generations feared the absence of authority, today we see "a fear of authority when it exists."

Some homileticians suggest that preachers should simply embrace this new worldview and surrender any claim to an authoritative message. Those who have lost confidence in the authority of the Bible as the Word of God are left with little to say and no authority for their message. Fred Craddock, among the most influential figures in recent homiletic thought, famously describes today's preacher "as one without authority." His portrait of the preacher's predicament is haunting:

The old thunderbolts rust in the attic while the minister tries to lead his people through the morass of relativities and proximate possibilities. No longer can the preacher presuppose the general recognition of his authority as a clergyman, or the authority of his institution, or the authority of Scripture.

Summarizing the predicament of the postmodern preacher, he relates that the preacher "seriously asks himself whether he should continue to serve up monologue in a dialogical world."

The obvious question to pose to Craddock's analysis is this: "If we have no authoritative message, why preach?" Without authority, the preacher and the congregation are involved in a massive waste of precious time. The very idea that preaching can be transformed into a dialogue between the pulpit and the pew indicates the confusion of our era.

Contrasted to this is the note of authority found in all true expository preaching. As Martyn Lloyd-Jones notes:

Any study of church history, and particularly any study of the great periods of revival or reawakening, demonstrates above everything else just this one fact: that the Christian

Church during all such periods has spoken with authority. The great characteristic of all revivals has been the authority of the preacher. There seemed to be something new, extra, and irresistible in what he declared on behalf of God.

The preacher dares to speak on behalf of God. He stands in the pulpit as a steward "of the mysteries of God" (1 Cor 4:1) and declares the truth of God's Word, proclaims the power of that Word, and applies the Word to life. This is an admittedly audacious act. No one should even contemplate such an endeavor without absolute confidence in a divine call to preach and in the unblemished authority of the Scriptures.

In the final analysis, the ultimate authority for preaching is the authority of the Bible as the Word of God. Without this authority, the preacher stands naked and silent before the congregation and the watching world. If the Bible is not the Word of God, the preacher is involved in an act of self-delusion or professional pretension.

Standing on the authority of Scripture, preaching declares a truth received, not a message invented. The teaching office is not an advisory role based in religious

> If the Bible is not the Word of God, the preacher is involved in an act of self-delusion or professional pretension.

expertise, but a prophetic function whereby God speaks to his people.

Authentic expository preaching is also marked by reverence. The congregation that gathered before Ezra and the other preachers demonstrated a love and reverence for the Word of God (Nch 8). When the book was read, the people stood up. This act of standing reveals the heart of the people and their sense of expectancy as the Word was read and preached.

Expository preaching requires an attitude of reverence on the part of the congregation. Preaching is not a dialogue, but it does involve at least two parties – the preacher and the congregation. The congregation's role in the preaching event is to hear, receive and obey the Word of God. In so doing, the church demonstrates reverence for the preaching and teaching of the Bible and understands that the sermon brings the Word of Christ near to the congregation. This is true worship.

Lacking reverence for the Word of God, many congregations are caught in a frantic quest for significance in worship. Christians leave worship services asking each other, "Did you get anything out of that?" Churches produce surveys to measure expectations for worship. "Would you like more music?" "What kind?" "How about drama?" "Is our preacher sufficiently creative?"

Expository preaching demands a very different set of questions. "Will I obey the Word of God?" "How must my thinking be realigned by Scripture?" "How must I change my behavior to be fully obedient to the Word?" These questions reveal submission to the authority of God and reverence for the Bible as his Word.

Likewise, the preacher must demonstrate his own reverence for God's Word by dealing truthfully and responsibly with the text. He must not be flippant or casual, much less dismissive or disrespectful. Of this we can be certain – no congregation will revere the Bible more than the preacher does.

Conclusion

If expository preaching is authoritative, and if it demands reverence, it must also be at the center of Christian worship. Worship properly directed to the honor and glory of God will find its center in the reading and preaching of the Word of God. Expository preaching cannot be assigned a supporting role in the act of worship – it must be central.

In the course of the Reformation, Luther's driving purpose was to restore preaching to its proper place in Christian worship. That same reformation is needed in American evangelicalism today. Expository preaching must once again be central to the life of the church and central to Christian worship. In the end, the church will not be judged by her Lord for

> Of this we can be certain – no congregation will revere the Bible more than the preacher does.

> Worship properly directed to the honor and glory of God will find its center in the reading and preaching of the Word of God.

the quality of her music but for the faithfulness of her preaching.

When today's evangelicals speak casually of the distinction between worship and preaching (meaning that the church will enjoy an offering of music before adding on a bit of preaching), they betray their misunderstanding of both worship and the act of preaching. Worship is not something we do before we settle down for the Word of God; it is the act through which the people of God direct all their attentiveness to hearing the one true and living God speak to his people and receive their praises. God is most beautifully praised when his people hear his Word, love his Word and obey his Word.

As in the Reformation, the most important corrective to our corruption of worship (and defense against the consumerist demands of the day) is to return expository preaching and the public reading of God's Word to their rightful primacy and centrality in worship. Only then will the "missing jewel" be truly rediscovered. ∞

This material was adapted from "Expository Preaching: Center of Christian Worship," in *Give Praise to God*, edited by Philip Graham Ryken, Derek W.H. Thomas, and J. Ligon Duncan III, copyright 2003, P & R Publishing, Phillipsburg, N.J.

It also appeared in *He Is Not Silent*, by R. Albert Mohler Jr., copyright 2008, Moody Publishers, Chicago, Ill.

THIS IS WAR

Expository Exorcism

Russell D. Moore

The scariest sound I've ever heard in my life was one of my children screaming, "Daddy!" And it came at a moment that was otherwise completely ordinary. I had been traveling with my wife and four small boys across the state of Tennessee. It happened to be one of those road trips where the shouts of, "He's touching me!" "He's sitting close to me!" "He's taking my Legos!" seemed constant. I was also getting calls about issues at the church or at the seminary where I work that needed my attention. It was just a long, exhausting day.

To top it off, we were driving in a rainstorm, so we pulled off the side of the interstate and found a hotel. And when I walked up to the front desk of the hotel, the young woman working looked remarkably like a woman I knew in college. And as we talked I found myself enjoying the conversation. There weren't any inappropriate thoughts, no inappropriate actions. Nothing happened that was in any way shady. I was just enjoying the conversation for a few minutes, talking about the high school football game going on down the street and about the rain storm. I was enjoying not being Pastor Moore or Dr. Moore or dad; I was enjoying just being a guy when suddenly I heard "Daddy!" And there was my four-year-old on a luggage cart, pushing it around like a train and yelling, "Daddy, look at this!" "Daddy, look what I can do!" And it scared me down to the core, not because anything was going to happen, but because I had forgotten who I was. I was in a bubble of illusion, and the illusion was frightening.

Evading Glory

This scene was so scary because this is exactly what the Scriptures say happens all the time with every single one of us: we enjoy living in

> We enjoy living in an illusion. But that illusion needs to be broken by the gospel.

an illusion. But that illusion needs to be broken by the gospel. This illusion is what Paul describes when he writes to the church at Corinth about blinded eyes, the veiled gospel and hard hearts. He's not saying that some kinds of people aren't going to receive the gospel. He's saying there is a universal, human condition among sinners whereby we seek to remain in that illusion and evade the light of the glory of the gospel of Christ. Looking at glory is painful for sinners. Looking at the light causes us to shrink back. And, like Adam and Eve in the garden, it causes us to hide from the presence of God, from the voice that breaks through and says, "Where are you?"

For those of you who preach, you need to know that the key element to good preaching is neither technique nor managing information, it's that you know what you're doing. Preaching in

Scripture and preaching among the churches of the Lord Jesus is not only communicating information. It is an act of exorcism. It's delivering people from the illusion in which they are held captive by the powers of darkness. When the gospel is preached, it's in a context where demonic beings are at work. And they serve the one whom Paul doesn't shrink back from calling "The god of this age, who has blinded the minds of unbelievers."

That illusion – the veil that hangs over the face, the hardening of the heart, the blindness of the spiritual eyes – is not just human depravity. It is not just some abstract concept. Personal beings actively use this illusion for the purpose of murder and destruction. So when you preach, you're engaging in spiritual warfare in the heavenly places because you're challenging the illusion propped up by the rulers and the principalities of this present darkness. That's what preaching is.

And that's the reason boring preaching isn't just ineffective, boring preaching is satanic. If all you do is allow people to hear the Word of God while evading it – even if you're as faithful to the text as possible – then your preaching is no better than Satan's, when he was faithful to the text in the wilderness and yet bypassed Christ.

When you stand up to preach, you must know what you're up against.

Ladder of Abstraction

Roy Peter Clark is a writer who tries to help people write fiction and journalism more effectively. He uses an image that rings true for preachers: the ladder of abstraction. At the top of this ladder are abstract ideas, universal human truths. And at the bottom of the ladder are concrete, particular, real life experiences.

Clark gives the example of a

> Preaching in Scripture and preaching among the churches of the Lord Jesus is not only communicating information. It is an act of exorcism.

Boring preaching isn't just ineffective, boring preaching is satanic.

school board gathering to discuss curricular changes. At the top of the ladder of abstraction is the idea that a literate people is good for the country. It's good for the citizens of the country to know how to read and to know how to govern themselves. At the bottom of the ladder is a little girl named Madison who isn't learning how to read in Mrs. Gallagher's second grade class.

The problem, according to Clark, is that most people in the school board don't talk about the universal truth at the top of the ladder, and they don't talk about the particular, identifiable situation at the bottom of the ladder. Instead, they stay in the middle of the ladder, where they talk about instructional units and curricular changes. They don't get at the root of what's happening.

I'm afraid that much of our preaching stays right in the middle of the ladder of abstraction, too. We never concretize what we say.

And because we don't, we never get to those universal, common longings and fears and rebellions and dilemmas of our listeners. We stay vague and abstract and boring. We allow people to remain in the illusion, and keep a distance from the voice of Christ in the Scriptures. People are able to move around it and move beside it and move behind it, but they never hear the liberating word from the liberating voice in the text.

Before you can preach to your people, and before you can address those who do not yet follow Christ, you need to understand that the people listening are experts at avoiding the Word of God. They are experts at evading the truth of Christ. People who couldn't find Hosea with a thumb tab still are experts at evading the Word of God because they've been doing this their entire lives, just as you and I did. When your preaching is functioning as exorcism, part of your job is to use the Word of God to tear down the illusions that you and your people construct.

Illustration: Drawing in Concrete

You can more effectively exorcise your listeners from those illusions by being more concrete with illustration. Sometimes we think of illustration as a mere pause in the flow of our argument, but that's not what illustration is about. Illustration is about spiritual warfare. It's about going behind enemy lines, behind the defense mechanisms in the heart, and attacking illusions with the sword of the Spirit, which is the Word of God. That's what happens, for instance, when Nathan confronts David. Had Nathan simply walked up to David and said, "You, sir, are an adulterer and you should not have slept with Bathsheba," David could have avoided the charge. David had likely found a way to justify his adultery with Bathsheba. He had already hardened his heart to that truth, and he would have been able to evade it. Instead, Nathan gives

> Sometimes we think of illustration as a mere pause in the flow of our argument. Illustration is about spiritual warfare.

a scenario that David identifies with and agrees with before he turns it around on him.

When you illustrate, you're refusing "to practice cunning," as Paul says. You're saying to your people, "I want to make sure you see what the Scripture says." When you preach, many of your listeners will be in despair, and some of them just can't believe that they're the kind of people that Jesus can save. But what you do when you illustrate is show them what things could be like, what their lives could look like.

It's kind of like Sesame Street. The most effective thing that Sesame Street did when it started was not teach people the alphabet. What Sesame Street did so effectively was put together a television show in the late 1960s and the early 1970s – in an era of George Wallace segregation, the Black Panther Party, Richard Nixon's "southern strategy" and race riots in South Boston – that presented a group of people from different races in the same neighborhood as equals. Sesame Street was contextualizing, but it was not contextualizing to the present, it was contextualizing to the future. They were saying, "This is what life could be like. This is not as impossible or crazy as you think, if you can just see what we're talking about, you can see a vision to aspire to."

That is what you do as you illustrate the Word of God. You're saying, "This is what it could be like if your life were transformed by the gospel. This is how the gospel could transform your envy, your lust, your despair, your hopelessness." You find those particular, concrete examples that people already understand, and you use them to display the big truth of what the gospel does through Jesus Christ.

A common tendency for preachers who want to use more effective illustrations is to find out all the things their people are reading and listening to, and to try to be informed on all of it. To some degree, it's helpful to know what's influencing the people in your community. But honestly, in order to illustrate well, it's better for you to read good fiction that gives insight into human nature than it is for you to read *The Hunger Games* or *The Da Vinci Code*. As you think through fiction and poetry and music, you'll start to grasp how human beings think and respond and react and live.

You've got to eavesdrop. You've got to listen to people's conversations while you're in line waiting for coffee. Sit down and ask people questions, even people

> As you illustrate the Word of God, you're saying, "This is what it could be like if your life were transformed by the gospel."

you don't know and people with whom you won't be able to build a relationship. Find out how people think, how they process, how they hear what you say, so that you speak and talk to real people in a way that they understand.

For the sake of your preaching, you need to be one-on-one with people in your congregation, hearing the kinds of ways your people understand the Word of God and the gospel. Knowing what's going on in and around your people will keep you from being, as Paul says, "ignorant of the designs of the serpent of Eden."

Application:
In Your Face
In order to be a more fruitful exorcist, the same concretizing needs to happen in your

application. You need application when you preach. The New Testament's letters all include a call for application, as did the teaching of Jesus. The problem is that some preachers think application consists of giving a list of four life principles to take home. There are people in the opposite direction who think application is always a call to cling to Christ, believe in Christ, believe the gospel, trust the gospel.

In biblical, gospel preaching, however, application is not all that different than illustration. When you apply – not just at the end of your message, but throughout – you say, "I'm talking to you." It's an act of love and kindness to say, "I know you don't think I'm talking to you, but I'm really and honestly talking to you." This means you need to spend time compassionately thinking about the ways your people are deceived and held in captivity by darkness. You need to love your

> You need to love your people enough to apply, and not with vagueness.

people enough to apply, and not with vagueness.

Sometimes we assume that if we speak vaguely, then everyone will get something from it, but that never works. Vagueness doesn't exorcise. You just sound like Charlie Brown's incomprehensible teacher. But when you address a particular, concrete situation, you're better able to get to the universal human truths that the gospel addresses. As you preach with the authority of Christ, you apply with concrete clarity so that your people can't misunderstand.

I had a guy come see me one time. He said, "I need to talk about my marriage. I think I may be in an unequally yoked situation." When I asked what he meant, he said, "Well, the way I interpret what the apostle Paul is saying is that, 'you ought not be unequally yoked with somebody who is spiritually immature.' And I'm married to a woman who's really, really immature as a believer. And it's frustrating to me because I'm trying to lead our family, but she is so carnal," he said. "She never prays, she never reads her Bible, she never shows any kind of spirituality to our kids. She sits around and watches these nasty programs on television. And, it's just really discouraging to me."

Then he said, "We have some theological issues too." When I asked him about those, he told me it was about the use of alcohol. I said, "Okay. A lot of people disagree about that. Tell me how it works out in your house."

He said, "Well, I believe it's okay to use alcohol moderately and she doesn't. And she objects to it when I do it."

I asked him what moderate use of alcohol looks like for him. He said, "Every night after I do family devotions, I drink a 12-pack of beer until I go to sleep." I said, "Let's talk about drunkenness and what Scripture says about that." And he said, "I've never been drunk! I've never been drunk in my life. I just drink the 12-pack of beer or whatever else is there until I go to sleep." I said, "Drinking until you pass out is drunkenness. I don't care who you are."

But what was amazing to me was that this guy wasn't trying to deceive me. He genuinely believed that his problem was a spiritually immature wife. And he was seeking a license from me to be able to go home and say to his wife, "You have got a serious problem."

But this guy's not unusual. I do that all the time, too. I constantly try to find a way to evade what the

You need to preach and apply so that they can't evade the truth.

Scripture says. We all do this, even the most mature among us. That means you need to preach and apply so that they can't evade the truth, and so they know exactly what you're saying and what you're not saying.

Pay attention to your people. If you are preaching the lordship of Jesus but you find a lot of genuine believers in your congregation who suddenly doubt that they're believers, then you're being misunderstood. If you're preaching the free grace of God but you find people are using that as license for a lifestyle of rebellion, you're being misunderstood.

Not everyone will hear with the heart, however. For some, your preaching will be an aroma of death to death, but to others, it will be an aroma of life to life (2 Cor 2:16). But you, by applying specifically and concretely, make sure that the Word is heard and understood.

Delivery: Get Thee Behind Me

If you're doing exorcism when you preach, then delivery matters. Delivery matters because you can falsify a statement simply by the way you say it. You can confuse people with your arguments by the way you argue. Boring preaching can actually enable your listeners to remain in the very illusions you're trying to destroy. Working on your delivery is not about being a peddler of the Word of God; it's about removing the distraction that comes from boring preachers. Sometimes, when we hear Paul's warning about people with itching ears who "will accumulate for themselves teachers to suit their own passions," (2 Tim 4:3) we assume that they must be piling up really skillful orators. So, we conclude, it must be more spiritual to come to the pulpit and say, "Well, here we are continuing our 35th week in our series of Philippians chapter one, verse two, part A. Here it is, let's move on through this." No!

When you preach and teach, you try to distract people from their captivity long enough to hear the voice that liberates and exorcises them from it. So, there must be a weightiness behind what you say. You must speak, plead and beg as though Jesus himself was

> Working on your delivery is not about being a peddler of the Word of God; it's about removing the distraction that comes from boring preachers.

pleading and begging through you, "Be reconciled to God." That will look different for different preachers. But if you're charged with adrenaline for the gospel, and with compassion for people held captive by the principalities and powers, and if you know that the voice of Jesus is what drives back the illusions and powers of satanic darkness, and that people hear the voice of Jesus when a text of Scripture is explained clearly, then you can't help but preach with a Galilean accent.

Pulpit Warfare

There was a woman who came to my congregation looking to be

baptized. I was talking with her and said, "How did you come to know the Lord Jesus?" She said, "I was watching a horror film." The woman, who was a single mom, said, "The baby was in bed. I was watching this movie and I got really creeped out. And I stayed creeped out all night long and into the next morning, so I wanted to get around a bunch of people so I wouldn't be creeped out. And I said, 'We're just going to go to church.'" While she was there, she heard the gospel, and she believed.

In a very real sense, her story is typical of every single one of us. We live in a demon-haunted universe, a horror show, and part of the task of your gospel preaching is to awaken people to the horror and offer them the freedom of the gospel that liberates and exorcises sinners from deception and illusion. You're not seeking simply to give them enough information so they make an informed decision. You're not trying to provide principles to help them make good choices. What you do through your preaching is show people the light of the glory of God in the face of Jesus, so that when the light breaks through from the text, the sheep of Christ will hear his voice and follow him (John 10:27). That's what preaching is. ∞

> Part of the task
> of your gospel
> preaching is to
> awaken people
> to the horror
> and offer them
> the freedom
> of the gospel.

A LIFE ABOVE REPROACH

Expository Living

Dan Dumas

When God called you out of your sin and despair, he did so with a purpose: holiness. He redeems people from the pit and intends for each and every one of them to be conformed to the image of his Son (Rom 8:29). God saves sinners to be holy. This was the case under the Old Covenant, when God brought Israel out of Egypt and made them "a kingdom of priests and a holy nation" (Ex 19:6). The same happens under the New Covenant. Paul says that God "chose us ... before the foundation of the world, that we should be holy and blameless before him" (Eph 1:4).

Holy Leadership, Holy People

If God demands holiness from all of his people, then it is extremely important that their leaders be holy. Rarely do people rise above their leaders; as the leaders go, so go the people.

God is emphatic about the character of those who lead his people. He gives a scathing rebuke of Israel's priests in Hosea 4:6-9 because they forgot the law of God. This forgetfulness resulted in the people's being "destroyed for lack of knowledge; because you (the priests) have rejected knowledge" (Hos 4:6). Jeremiah records a similar rebuke of Israel's spiritual leaders, where the Lord pronounces, "Woe to the shepherds who destroy and scatter the sheep of my pasture" (Jer 23:1)! Likewise, the writer of Hebrews says that leaders will give account before God for their stewardship of those under their care (Heb 13:17).

> God is emphatic about the character of those who lead his people.

The good of those under authority depends on the faithfulness of those in authority. God gave elders to lead the church, and if elders are unfaithful in their lives and leadership, their people suffer.

A Noble Office

God calls elders to lead, feed and protect the church, and, while people can legitimately disagree about how elders should function, there should be no debate that elders must be men of character. Paul gives a list of qualifications for church eldership in 1 Timothy 3, and almost all of the qualifications have to do with a man's character. Paul's list is not exhaustive, but it still gives an opportunity for elders and those aspiring to eldership to examine themselves against the brilliant light of Scripture.

New Testament scholar D.A. Carson observes, "Elders are not a higher class of Christians. What is required of all believers is peculiarly required of the leaders of believers." Elders may not be required to abide by a stricter moral code than other Christians, but there are unique repercussions if their morality fails. In other words, there isn't a higher standard for the character of elders, but there is a higher accountability.

Paul knew that the character and conduct of an elder is critical. He knew that a pastor who acts in stark contrast with what he preaches will wreak havoc on his people. He knew that an office as critical as church elder demands a man who is serious about his life. He knew that a noble occupation demands a noble character.

This kind of character comes as a result of ruthlessly fighting the daily war, which is full of little battles along the way. Pastor Kevin DeYoung comments, "Holiness is the sum of a million little things and not one heroic act." You will fight against the world, flesh and devil on a daily basis whether you like it or not, and if you don't attack temptation, it will attack you. As John Owen noted, you need to "be killing sin or it will be killing you."

> There isn't a higher standard for the character of elders, but there is a higher accountability.

Above Reproach

Paul insists on an elder's holiness in five major life categories: public, marital, family, personal and doctrinal. Paul sums up these areas with two words: above reproach. This is Paul's way of saying that the elder should have no loopholes in his character. Being above reproach means you have unimpeachable character, but it doesn't mean you're flawless. There's a difference between having a bad day and having a bad year; the elder should live in such a way as to be accusation-free and without any sustained or legitimate patterns of sin.

When he played in the National Hockey League, Wayne Gretzky, widely considered the best hockey player of all time, did his best to live in a way that upheld his reputation, as well as that of his team and the N.H.L. He was held in such high regard that when he was charged (falsely, it turns out) in a gambling scandal, some of Gretzky's former teammates and coaches quickly came to his defense. They recalled how he carried himself with impeccable care, always aware that he was a watched man. He never walked down the streets alone, lest anyone get the wrong idea. He was never alone in an elevator with a woman other than his wife, he didn't stay out late with teammates and he tried to drive the speed limit. Gretzky did his best to be above reproach with his lifestyle because he knew people were watching.

Elders could learn something from Gretzky. The church is infinitely more worthy of careful living from her leaders than the N.H.L. Elders aren't merely protecting their own image and reputation; they're protecting the image and reputation of the church and of her Lord. The damage done by a pastor's moral failure surpasses any PR mess a sports league might find itself in.

Because God demands such character in those who lead his church, it is imperative that we regularly sit at the feet of Paul in 1 Timothy 3 to let him instruct us and remind us of those demands. So let's begin.

1 Timothy 3:1-7
HUSBAND OF ONE WIFE (V.2)

The first qualification for eldership in the local church is not charisma, not visionary leadership, not captivating oration. The first qualification is faithfulness, and the first place to look for this is a man's marriage. He won't be a faithful elder if he isn't first a faithful husband.

An elder must be enduringly faithful to his wife and have eyes for her alone. If you suffer from "wandering eye syndrome," you need to nip it in the bud. Those kinds of habits can turn into a ministry-destroying monster if left unchecked.

Perhaps you're curious about the assumption that an elder be male. I'm making the assumption on the basis of Paul's explicit instruction in 1 Timothy 2 that a woman not teach or "exercise authority over a man" (1 Tim 2:12). That's why Paul can give the gender-specific requirement just five verses later that an elder be the husband of one wife.

We know that faithfulness is a requirement for eldership, but is marriage required? No, but the same faithfulness demanded in marriage needs to be a mark of your singleness.

Can divorced men be elders? Each situation calls for wisdom, but Paul appears to be commenting on the quality of an elder's marriage rather than the quantity. What matters is that the man in question has an established pattern of fidelity, and that he's proven himself to be a one-woman man.

Conversely, it's possible to be married to one woman but not be a one-woman man by Paul's standards. If a man continually looks at other women – in real life or on the computer – or if he harbors inappropriate thoughts and feelings toward another woman, then he has proven himself to be disqualified for eldership. Elders, love your wives and devote yourselves to them.

SOBER-MINDED (V.2)

Sober-mindedness should be valued and pursued by all Christians. The New Testament exhorts sober-mindedness among elders, elders' wives (1 Tim 3:11), older men (Titus 2:2), and Christians generally (1 Peter 1:13, 4:7, 5:8). If it's so important, then what is it? Sober-mindedness is a disposition that gives serious attention to one's doctrine and life. If you're an elder, or want to be an elder, you need to take seriously not only your doctrine and life, but how it makes an impact on those under your leadership.

Elder, you need to cultivate sober-mindedness in all aspects of your life. You need to cultivate moderation in your life rather than excess. You need to be sensible in your decisions rather than rash and impulsive. You need to make a habit of mature, clear and serious thinking rather than having bouts of boyish, immature, frat-boy kinds of behavior and thought.

When you were a child, you could speak and think and reason as such, but as a man, you need to put away childish ways and think like the sober-minded man God created you to be, and that God's people need you to be (1 Cor 13:11).

SELF-CONTROLLED (V.2)

Self-control is a big deal in Paul's mind. It's the final fruit of the Spirit listed in Galatians 5:22-23. Paul isn't the only one who deemed it important, the Book of Proverbs also warns that "A man without self-control is like a city broken into and left without walls" (Prov 25:28). In a culture where indulging any and all desires is encouraged, it is imperative that your people see you practice and display self-mastery. If you don't have self-control, it's not likely that your people will, either. If you don't have self-control, you leave your church as vulnerable as a city without walls.

> It is imperative that your people see you practice and display self-mastery.

RESPECTABLE (V.2)

Every man craves respect, whether it's from his wife, his boss, his children or his dog. Men, spend less time making sure everyone gives you the respect you think you deserve, and spend more time living a life that earns it. Put order and discipline into your life. Exercise dominion in the areas God has entrusted to you. Live with such a forceful character that even your opponents and enemies respect you.

HOSPITABLE (V.2)

Do people view your home as a refuge? As an elder and pastor, your home should be a place where fellow Christians come and receive refreshment and encouragement. Hospitality in the first century wasn't so much about getting together to watch football and eat food as it was about survival. An elder's home was, and still should be, a place of respite, a place where faith is strengthened, where fellow Christians and traveling missionaries can rest.

Your home isn't only for Christians, it should be a place where skeptics and unbelievers come and witness the gospel in action. You need to love your wife and raise your children in a way that commends the gospel. This doesn't mean your family life is perfect, or your house is a show room, but you're still called to use your home and resources to bless Christians, unbelievers and strangers (1 Pet 4:9; Heb 13:2).

ABLE TO TEACH (V.2)

The ability to articulate Christian doctrine should not be unique to elders. The ability to teach, however, is a unique requirement for elders.

A man of stellar character can be disqualified by an inability to teach. He should not only be able to teach clearly the doctrines of the faith, but also defend the church against false teaching (Titus 1:9). When pastors "contend for the faith that was once for all delivered to the saints" (Jude 3), they must be able to articulate and refute, to contend and defend.

As an elder, you're both a teacher and apologist. The ability to teach is not exclusively exercised from the pulpit; there are countless ways to teach your people both formally and informally. What matters is that you're ready to articulate and defend the faith in season and out of season.

NOT A DRUNKARD (V.3)

"It is not for kings to drink wine, or for rulers to take strong drink, lest they drink and forget what has been decreed" (Prov 31:4-5). It

> Your people are looking to you for an example of how to walk in a manner worthy of the gospel.

seems obvious, but pastors can't be drunkards. God commands that all Christians "not get drunk with wine…but be filled with the Spirit" (Eph 5:18). You can't be mastered by both wine and the Spirit, it's one or the other.

You need to use wisdom in your use of alcohol, considering the interests of others as greater than your own (Phil 2:4), lest you cause them to stumble. Remember, your people are looking to you for an example of how to walk in a manner worthy of the gospel.

NOT VIOLENT BUT GENTLE (V.3)

As an elder, hopefully you're not in regular physical altercations with your people when they irritate you. If you've got a short fuse and your frustration comes with physical manifestations, then you're not qualified to shepherd the flock. When your sheep bite, you can't bite back. Instead, you need to grow in gentleness and learn what it means to be quick to forgive.

Your gentleness needs to be visible in your instruction of others. Model yourself after Paul, who entreated the Corinthians "by the meekness and gentleness of Christ," (2 Cor 10:1), and who told Timothy to correct his opponents "with gentleness" (2 Tim 2:25).

Gentleness also needs to be visible when you receive criticism. Do you become defensive when you receive criticism, or do you respond with humility and an honest belief that "faithful are the wounds of a friend" (Prov 27:6)?

Whether you're receiving criticism, or you're teaching, refuting, rebuking, defending and training in righteousness, it all needs to be laden with gentleness.

NOT QUARRELSOME (V.3)

Elders are called to refute false teachers, but they are not called to go around looking for a fight. Do you love to argue? Do you love to be right? Do you love to argue until everyone thinks you're right? If so, then marvel at the Lord Jesus, who never engaged in debate for the sake of debating or belittling others. He only ever opened his mouth for the purpose of teaching, leading and shepherding. Even in his harshest rebukes, he had in mind the good of those around him. Elder, protect the flock, but don't go around looking for wolves to fight.

NOT A LOVER OF MONEY (V.3)

Some people think that being in ministry, with the simple lifestyle that often comes with it, will render a love of money irrelevant. But that's not so. You can simultaneously be poor and greedy.

If you struggle with greed, you need to give more of it away. The best way to stop loving money is to attack it with aggressive generosity. Your money is not your own. You can't call your people to lay up treasures in heaven while you're anxious about building and protecting yours on earth.

MANAGING HIS OWN HOUSEHOLD (V.4)

The qualification that an elder manage his household well is crucial. There is no better way to examine a man's leadership

---

HOW TO IDENTIFY POTENTIAL ELDERS

Identifying and appointing elders is of chief importance in healthy churches (Titus 1:5). To start the process, the slow, intentional, rigorous and biblically informed examination must be defined clearly. Ask the hard question up front. Does he have an,

- Unimpeachable character: are all of the qualifications of 1 Timothy 3 and Titus 1 true of him right now?

- Unquestionable commitment: is he willing to go the extra-mile and do the heavy lifting of pastoral oversight?

- Undeniable competency: is he able to handle the Scriptures (Titus 1:9)?

---

qualities and evaluate the long-term results of his leadership than to enter his home. The home is a microcosm of the church, and if you can't pastor the people in your home, you won't be able to pastor the people in your church. If your wife is hesitant about your fitness for ministry, then you should be, too. If you "succeed" at church but fail at home, then you fail. Period.

Does this qualification mean that your children must be believers? Titus 1:6 says the children of a potential elder should be "believers and not open to the charge of debauchery or insubordination." The King James Version says that an elder's children need to be "faithful." The translation could go either way, so it comes down to interpretation. Can Paul really require something that only God can ensure? Doesn't it make more sense that Paul would require that an elder's children be a positive

If your wife is hesitant about your fitness for ministry, then you should be, too.

testimony to his leadership? Paul seems to be saying in Titus 1:6 that an elder must be above reproach, and his kids must be under his authority.

Whatever your conclusion, be sure that you love your wife and raise your kids in a way that testifies to your trustworthiness.

NOT A NOVICE (V.6)

The elder is called to exposit and apply the Scriptures to the lives of his people, and that ability develops and deepens with time and practice. The longer a man walks with God and trusts him through trials, the more apt that man will be to speak truth into people's lives. It takes time for trials to result in a faith tested with genuineness (1 Pet 1:6-7).

If someone is a new Christian or an immature Christian, he is unfit to be an elder. When a new believer is thrust into a place of leadership, a train wreck is sure to follow. With premature leadership comes conceit, and with conceited leadership comes wounded people, and with wounded people comes a damaged gospel witness.

WELL THOUGHT OF BY OUTSIDERS (V.7)

The list of qualifications began with the call to be above reproach, and like a bookend, it ends with a call to be above reproach to those outside the church. An elder must have good rapport with unbelievers in the community. If you don't live that way, Paul says you're leading yourself into a snare of the devil (1 Tim 3:7).

If you plan to be well thought of by outsiders, your life needs to match your role as an elder. That doesn't mean you don't mess up. The mark of true faith, as pastor John Piper says, is not that you're perfect, but that you fight. You must be actively and aggressively engaged in grace-induced progressive sanctification. You better know where your weaknesses lie because the devil most certainly does. Keep close watch on and attack those weaknesses. If you don't, those little inconsistencies will become chains that bind you and may eventually disqualify you.

Conclusion

If you're an elder, you are a hunted man (1 Pet 5:8). You are a target for slander, scandal and Satan, and being on the frontlines of ministry guarantees you will get blood on your uniform. So, walk carefully. You need to be consistently taking inventory of your life and identifying any red flags.

If you're an elder, the overall quality of your life and faith

> The overall quality of an elder's life and faith should be worth exporting to others.

should be worth exporting to others. Paul encourages Timothy to do just that by setting "an example in speech, in conduct, in love, in faith, in purity" (1 Tim 4:12). "Some men build careers. Others erect empires. But the rarest of men leave legacies," said Steve Lawson. Leave a legacy of godliness the way Paul did, who had the audacity to command people to imitate him as he imitated Christ (1 Cor 11:1, Phil 3:17).

If you're an elder or pastor in your church, you've got to live a life worth imitating.

If you're an elder, you hold a noble office that demands a noble character. ∞

— PREACH THE WORD —

Fling him into his office. Tear the "Office" sign from the door and nail on the sign, "Study." Take him off the mailing list. Lock him up with his books and his typewriter and his Bible. Slam him down on his knees before texts and broken hearts and the lives of a superficial flock and a holy God.

Force him to be the one man in our surfeited communities who knows about God. Throw him into the ring to box with God until he learns how short his arms are. Engage him to wrestle with God all the night through. And let him come out only when he's bruised and beaten into being a blessing.

Shut his mouth forever spouting remarks, and stop his tongue forever tripping lightly over every nonessential. Require him to have something to say before he dares break the silence. Bend his knees in the lonesome valley.

Burn his eyes with weary study. Wreck his emotional poise with worry for God. And make him exchange his pious stance for a humble walk with God and man. Make him spend and be spent for the glory of God. Rip out his telephone. Burn up his ecclesiastical success sheets.

Put water in his gas tank. Give him a Bible and tie him to the pulpit. And make him preach the Word of the living God!

Test him. Quiz him. Examine him. Humiliate him for his ignorance of things divine. Shame him for his good comprehension of finances, batting averages and political infighting. Laugh at his frustrated effort to play psychiatrist. Form a choir and raise a chant and haunt him with it night and day – "Sir, we would see Jesus."

When at long last he dares assay the pulpit, ask him if he has a word from God. If he does not, then dismiss him. Tell him you can read the morning paper and digest the television commentaries, and think through the day's superficial problems, and manage the community's weary drives, and bless the sordid baked potatoes and green bean, ad infinitum, better than he can.

Command him not to come back until he's read and reread, written and rewritten, until he can stand up, worn and forlorn, and say, "Thus saith the Lord."

Break him across the board of his ill-gotten popularity. Smack him hard with his own prestige. Corner him with questions about God. Cover him with demands for celestial wisdom. And give him no escape until he's back against the wall of the Word.

And sit down before him and listen to the only word he has left – God's Word. Let him be totally ignorant of the down-street gossip, but give him a chapter and order him to walk around it, camp on it, sup with it and come at last to speak it backward and forward, until all he says about it rings with the truth of eternity.

And when he's burned out by the flaming Word, when he's consumed at last by the fiery grace blazing through him, and when he's privileged to translate the truth of God to man, finally transferred from earth to heaven, then bear him away gently and blow a muted trumpet and lay him down softly. Place a two-edged sword in his coffin, and raise the tomb triumphant. For he was a brave soldier of the Word. And ere he died, he had become a man of God.

– Anonymous, cited in John MacArthur's *Rediscovering Expository Preaching*.

IN SEASON AND OUT OF SEASON

Expository Readiness

Donald S. Whitney

I have a confession to make: I never feel fully prepared to preach. In fact, I'm not sure I know what it would mean to be fully prepared to preach. I suppose it might mean coming to the pulpit with a complete manuscript thoroughly highlighted in several colors. It would mean I had the sermon so internalized and was so familiar with it that the manuscript would be unnecessary. I would have practiced it out loud in the very pulpit in which I'm about to preach at least once. Before all this, I would have studied the text thoroughly. I would have consulted and pondered every commentary and reference book that I deemed important. I would be refreshed by a full night of sleep. I would have prayed as long as I wanted and come away with a sense of the unction of the Holy Spirit. I would have emerged from an intoxicating time of worship. If that is what it means to be prepared, then I've never been fully prepared to preach in my life.

There is a broader sense, however, in which the preacher is to be prepared. You could consider it from several perspectives. There is the call of the preacher, there is the education and training of the preacher, and, of course, there is the weekly preparation of the preacher for the pulpit. But I'm not concerned with any of those at the moment. I'm concerned with the ongoing preparation of the preacher. You might say I'm concerned with obeying Paul's command in 2 Timothy 4:2 to stay ready in season and out of season. How do you do that? How do you stay ready in light of our inability to be fully prepared? How do you do that when people, without consulting your schedule, inconveniently decide to die on Friday or decide to have some major surgery on your most

I'm concerned with obeying Paul's command to stay ready in season and out of season. How do you do that?

important day of sermon prep?

In answer to that question, I find these words from preacher, college president and hymn writer Samuel Davies to be an encouragement. After hearing the legendary George Whitefield preach, he said,

> It became clear to me quite soon in the service that Mr. Whitefield must have had an exceptionally busy week; obviously he had not had time to prepare his sermon properly. From the standpoint of construction and ordering of thought it was very deficient and defective; it was a poor sermon. But the unction that attended it was such that I would gladly risk the rigors of shipwreck in the Atlantic many times over in order to be there just to come under its gracious influence (Lloyd-Jones, *Puritans*, 123-4).

Davies is not advocating laziness in preparation. In fact, if you plan on regularly slacking in preparation and merely attempting to speak with unction to make up for it, then do us a favor and leave the ministry, will you?

Davies is not advocating laziness in preparation, but there are times when life happens and the preacher is less prepared than he would wish and yet is still able to deliver a powerful sermon.

Unction is neither a reward for hard work, nor something God owes you, but it is good to know how to be in a position where we may, by faith, expect such unction even when our preparation isn't complete. Paul tells us how to do this in 1 Timothy 4:16, where he exhorts Timothy to "keep a close watch on yourself and on the teaching. Persist in this, for by so doing you will save both yourself and your hearers." If we obey Paul's exhortation, we'll find ourselves in a much better position when our preparation isn't quite there. The key is to take heed of Paul's exhortations, so let's start there.

The Exhortations

PAY ATTENTION TO YOUR LIFE
The first imperative of 1 Timothy 4:16 is to "keep a close watch on yourself." Why does Paul say

The first priority of a man of God is to be a godly man.

this? Because the first priority of a man of God is to be a godly man. Robert Murray M'Cheyne, the great Scottish preacher of the 1830s, said, "The greatest thing I can give my people is my own personal holiness." How do we cultivate that in our lives? We don't pull ourselves up by our own spiritual bootstraps to become more like Jesus, but that doesn't mean we have nothing to do.

Our role is to use God-given means in the pursuit of holiness, and those means are the personal and interpersonal spiritual disciplines found in Scripture. But the disciplines are never an end in and of themselves; they're for the pursuit of godliness. The purpose of any spiritual discipline is to be like Jesus. We don't memorize Scripture to put notches on our Bible. We don't share the gospel to boast about how many people we've witnessed to that week. We don't fast in order to say how often we fast, or pray to say how many hours we prayed. We practice any and all of those disciplines to be like Jesus. That is a large part of how we watch our lives, according to 1 Timothy 4:16.

Of all the spiritual disciples exhorted in Scripture (such as personal and corporate worship, evangelism, service, stewardship of time and money, journaling, fasting and silence and solitude, among others) the most important are the disciplines of the Word and the discipline of prayer. Ministers should have the same priorities today as the Apostles did in Acts 6:4 – a devotion to prayer and the ministry of the Word. Do your people know you as a man of the Word and a man of prayer? Are you known for the habitual reading, hearing, studying, memorizing, meditating and applying of Scripture? Are you known for spending time on your knees pleading with God? You need to be doing these things if you're a gospel minister.

The disciplines are the God-given means for every Christian to grow in grace, and ministers need them as much as anyone, and perhaps more. Ordination does not make you a godly man. Just being in the ministry will not make you holy. If you're not careful, your familiarity with the ministry could make you callous to the things of God, it could anesthetize your awe of God. The ministry can be the means of making you more unlike Christ if you don't watch your life. It can foster political maneuvering and infighting. It can foster greed. It can foster power plays. It can foster so much that is antithetical to Christ-likeness, and the only way to keep that from happening is to do what this passage says: watch your life. And you do that through the rightly motivated practice of the spiritual disciplines.

Richard Baxter was an English Puritan preacher, writer and pastor extraordinaire, and he wrote on this same text in his book *The Reformed Pastor*. In it he lists eight reasons we need to pay close attention to our lives: First, pay close attention to your life because you have a heaven to win or lose, just like everybody else. Have you ever wondered how

The ministry can be the means of making you more unlike Christ if you don't watch your life.

RICHARD BAXTER'S EIGHT REASONS
TO WATCH YOUR LIFE

1. You have heaven to win or lose;
2. You're depraved with sinful inclinations;
3. You're exposed to greater temptations than others;
4. People are watching you, and they'll be there to observe your fall;
5. There's more hypocrisy involved when you sin;
6. Your work requires more grace than others;
7. The honor of Christ lies on you more than on others; and
8. The success of your labors depends on it.

many men there are who once warned people of hell from the pulpit who are now experiencing it? Who once warned of the wrath of God who are now underneath it? God is no respecter of persons. He does not save us because we are ministers or because we preach sermons or do good things for the church. You need to make sure of your calling and election as much as anybody (2 Pet 1:10).

Second, pay close attention to your life because you also have a depraved nature and sinful inclinations. Preachers can be as prideful or lustful or unbelieving or self-seeking or greedy as anyone else. And we're no less sinful because people now call us "reverend" or because we lead

worship services. No title can kill sinful inclinations. There are people, unfortunately, who go into ministry thinking, "Perhaps if I dedicate my life in service to God he will kill my sinful inclination," but that won't happen.

Third, pay close attention to your life because you are exposed to greater temptations than others. You think you know what spiritual warfare is until you go into the ministry. Satan works harder against those who lead the people of God. It is the same principle as in war, when the opposition would try to take down the officers first. Why? Because if the officers fall while leading their men in a charge, it greatly demoralizes the troops.

Fourth, pay close attention to your life because you have many eyes on you and there will be many to observe your fall. The media loves a scandal, and the public's eyes are irresistibly drawn to watch a fall from grace. And what is true on a national scale with nationally-known men is equally true on a local level with you. The town always remembers the preacher who falls. The church never forgets. The children and the teenagers are left questioning. Young Christians become disillusioned. The unconverted always have a target for their scoffing. Your community knows when you fall. Your fellow pastors know when you fall. The neighbors you have witnessed to will know that you fall. You have to tell your church what you've done. You have to tell your wife. You have to explain it to your children. You have to tell your extended family, and to those you've been praying for and witnessing to through the years. Pay close attention to your life.

Fifth, pay close attention to your life because your sins have what Baxter called "more heinous aggravations" than other men's. In other words, our sins are more serious because we have more light. We sin against more light than others. We know more of God's truth and we know it better than other people do, so there is more hypocrisy involved. We have stood and preached against the very sins we then commit. So pay close attention to your life.

Sixth, pay close attention to your life because your work requires greater grace than other men's. It takes marvelous grace to preach the great truths of the gospel, to lead the people of God, to lead in the work of the kingdom, to fight against the work of Satan and to rescue people from the path of hell. This requires more grace than other things you could be doing with your life.

Seventh, pay close attention to your life because the honor of Christ is on the line with you more than with other men. Judas' betrayal and Peter's denial were worse offenses than the fickle Jerusalem crowd that hailed Jesus on Sunday and called for his death on Friday because those

You think you know what spiritual warfare is until you go into the ministry.

two were closer to Christ. The closer you are to Christ, and the more closely you are identified with him, the greater potential you have for dishonoring him. You probably have greater potential to dishonor Christ than anyone else in your community. Can you imagine anything worse than unbelievers talking about your sins and laughing at the gospel because of what you've done? I hope that makes you shudder. I pray that God would kill me before he would allow me to be caught in something like that, for I know that like King David, I am capable of great, Christ-dishonoring sins.

Eighth, pay close attention to your life because the success of your labor depends on it. Can you expect to be fruitful if you're not serious about the things you preach? Will you be blessed in the care of the souls of others if you're careless with your own? So pay close attention to your life.

The honor of Christ is on the line with you more than other men.

AND TO YOUR TEACHING

Pay close attention not only to yourself but also to your teaching. This is the second imperative in 1 Timothy 4:16. My observation is that most ministers aren't doing this. They don't talk about it. They don't go to conferences about it. They don't read it. If they're paying close attention to anything, it is their methods and psychology. What's the result of this? Less biblical fidelity. Less interest in truth. Less seriousness. Less depth.

Neglecting doctrine results in less capacity to offer a compelling alternative to the thinking of our generation. I often hear the excuse that pastors aren't studying theology because they're too busy trying to reach more people. Ironically, this pursuit of identification often comes with a corresponding loss of communication. We put forth all this effort to make people feel comfortable and at home so that they don't feel the difference between life in Christ and life without Christ. The problem is that it is supposed to be different when you come to Christ. That is the point.

Maybe you think doctrine is unimportant, or maybe you're so gifted that you don't think you need it. Chances are you're not

Chances are you're not as gifted as was Timothy – Paul's hand-picked disciple – and Paul told Timothy to pay attention to doctrine. That means you need it, too.

as gifted as was Timothy – Paul's hand-picked disciple – and Paul told Timothy to pay attention to doctrine. That means you need it, too. Doctrine is what keeps you going when your people are dying – or it seems they're trying to make sure you do. Doctrine is what draws us near to God and keeps fresh our love for and awe of God. It was after 11 chapters of Paul's most densely packed, closely argued, systematic presentation of doctrine that he leapt into doxology:

Oh, the depth of the riches and wisdom and knowledge of God! How unsearchable are his judgments and how inscrutable his ways! For from him and through him and to him are all things. To him be glory forever. Amen (Rom 11:33, 36).

Paul was never more doxological than when he was his most theological. Theology is what nourished Paul's heart, and it will nourish yours. Pay attention to your life and to your doctrine.

I experienced this very thing one year early in my pastoral ministry. It was mid-December and I realized, "It's time for the Christmas sermon. How am I going to present freshly the Christmas message everyone knows so well?" I didn't know what to preach – maybe some obscure text from Ezekiel in hopes that it would not sound so predictable. I decided, instead, to do some fresh reading on the doctrine of the incarnation.

As I read the Scriptures and the other resources I had on the doctrine, I found myself so refreshed and so captivated by the glory of the incarnation that I had too much to say in one sermon. After reading all that glorious theology, I was able to convey some of the splendor of the incarnation and address some common misconceptions about it, and as I was preaching

I could see the circuit breakers going off in people's minds. Many who presumed they had the Christmas story down pat began to realize they could not get their minds completely around this magnificent, God-sized truth – which was just the point I wanted to communicate. I wanted them to see the glorious wonder of the incarnation, the greatness of this doctrine that God became fully man. And it was all because God got my attention and reminded me that I needed to keep a close watch on my teaching.

If Timothy needed to pay attention to his doctrine, then you and I need to pay close attention to our doctrine throughout our lives. Someone has said that every doctrine of Scripture is shallow enough for a child to walk in and deep enough for an elephant to swim in, and that is part of what it means to "continue in what you have learned," as Paul instructs in 2 Timothy 3:14. Have you learned about the incarnation? Good! Now continue learning the incarnation. You think you know the gospel, and justification by faith? Good! Now, continue learning and proclaiming them.

PERSIST IN THIS

The third imperative in 1 Timothy 4:16 is "persist in this." What is "this?" "This" is paying attention to your life and doctrine. When Paul departed from the Ephesian elders in Acts 20, he told them through tears to "pay careful attention to yourselves and to all the flock." The way to protect the flock is to pay attention to doctrine, lest they be led astray by false teaching. He said the same thing to Titus in the exhortation to "show yourself in all respects to be a model of good works, and in your teaching show integrity" (Titus 2:7). That is just another way of saying pay attention to your life and to your doctrine. He said it over and over. That is your ongoing preparation as a minister in God's church.

How do we make sure we "show integrity" in our teaching, that we have purity of doctrine? At the very least, we must keep studying it and persisting in it. A few years ago I was preaching at a pastor's conference about the importance of doctrine and a pastor told me that when he reached the age of 40 he assumed he wouldn't need to learn anymore, he just needed to apply what he learned. That is not persevering in doctrine. That is not being like Paul.

The last chapter Paul ever wrote includes an instruction for Timothy to "bring the cloak that I left with Carpus at Troas, also the books, and above all the parchments" (2 Tim 4:13). He was about to die and he wanted books. He wanted to study doctrine. If there is one man in history who didn't need to study doctrine, wouldn't it be Paul, the man who wrote the doctrine we study? And if he needed to study, wouldn't you think he'd at least loosen up a bit as he is about to die? At this point, Paul is probably the most mature Christian who has ever lived. He knows more doctrine than any of us. He has been inspired to

> The last chapter Paul ever wrote includes an instruction for Timothy to bring the books and the parchments. He was about to die and he wanted books. He wanted to study doctrine.

write it. He has been taken to heaven to see the culmination of all theology (2 Cor 12:1-10). Paul knows doctrine. But he wanted his last thoughts to be his best thoughts, directed toward the pure and inerrant Word of God. He was a man who persevered and grew in doctrine until his last day.

A friend of mine once told me a story about his seminary graduation rehearsal. If you've ever been to one, you know they tend to last awhile, so my friend decided to use the time to read a new book about sanctification that had been making a lot of noise. So he brought the book and a couple of systematic theology books to read during the rehearsal. As he read, the guy on his right looked at him and said, "Do you still have a paper you have to finish?" Before he could answer, the guy on the other side jumped in and said, "Do you still have a final to take before you can graduate tomorrow?" And to both of them he answered, "No." They sat there bewildered: "Then why are you reading that?"

And my friend said, "Because I want to understand better the doctrine of sanctification." And this newly-minted pastor on his right says, "Not me. I'm never reading another theology book again." And the preacher on his left added, "I'm not going to waste my time on that stuff anymore. I'm just going to go out and preach Jesus."

So there sat my friend, ridiculed for studying theology at his very graduation from a theological seminary. How would you like to sit under a pastor who had that kind of attitude toward the things of God? How would you like to have a surgeon who had that kind of attitude toward learning after medical school? Pastors are physicians of souls, which means we should at least take as much care in the knowledge and doctrines of our calling as physicians do in the latest medical advances. We need to persevere both in devotion and doctrine.

The Promises

Paul follows those three exhortations with two promises for those who continually prepare themselves: "for by so doing you

---

A PASTOR'S (OR PROSPECTIVE PASTOR'S) SELF-EXAMINATION

1. Do you believe God knows the best way for us to win souls?
If you're a minister of the gospel, don't devote yourself primarily to demographics and data, devote yourself to disciplines and doctrine, for by this you will save yourself and your hearers.

2. Are you devoted to the disciplines of godly living?
If you strip away your title would you be able to testify to your growth in grace? Would others see it by observing you? You have to be a model for God's people.

3. Are you devoted to developing in doctrine?
If, as a pastor, you have no taste for studying doctrine, no heart for it, then you've misunderstood your call. The bulwark against the eroding tide in your church is the pulpit. Strong churches have godly men preaching the truth of God.

> This is the heart of Paul's church growth strategy, to be a godly man living like Jesus, and paying close attention to the doctrine he preached.

will save both yourself and your hearers" (1 Tim 4:16). The first promise states that as you do this – as you pay attention to your life and your doctrine and persist in doing so – you will ensure your own salvation. Paul understood that there is such a thing as self-deception. There is such a thing as false assurance and, though he had actually been taken to heaven and had seen miracles performed through his own hands and had seen multitudes converted by God through his ministry, he still knew that none of that guaranteed anything. Even the apostle Paul realized the only way to ensure that the reality of self-deception

doesn't happen is to stay close to Christ, to pay attention to your life and to your doctrine.

The second promise states that by watching your life and doctrine, and persisting in these things, you will also save "your hearers." This is the only verse in the Bible that declares "do this" and you can be sure that people will be saved. You don't usually hear that kind of thing at a church growth and evangelism conference, but this is what God uses to draw people to himself. This was the heart of Paul's evangelism. This is the heart of Paul's church growth strategy, to be a godly man living like Jesus, and paying close attention to the doctrine he preached.

Make this the heart and the goal of your ministry. Keep watch on yourself. Run hard after Christ, decide to know nothing but him and him crucified. Make his story the content of your preaching and praying and leading. Keep watch on your doctrine, continue to grow in the knowledge of God. Persevere in these things. Fight hard. Make it your life goal to do these things, believing the promises that accompany them, so that when the end draws near you can say with Paul, "I have fought the good fight, I have finished the race, I have kept the faith" (2 Tim 4:7). ∞

MIGHTY IN THE SCRIPTURES

One of the greatest Southern Baptist forbears is John A. Broadus, who with James P. Boyce, William Williams and Basil Manly Jr., founded The Southern Baptist Theological Seminary in 1859. The fledgling seminary closed during the Civil War and restarted afterwards with only seven students, and four faculty who took no salary.

Only one student enrolled in Broadus' homiletics course. The student was blind and was very sick and actually died within two years of graduation. Broadus was one of the brightest, best-trained minds of his time, and he was also devoted to doctrine. In fact he loved it so much he couldn't be slack in teaching even one blind, sickly student. Broadus prepared so well that afterward he collected his lectures and they were published in a book called *On the Preparation and Delivery of Sermons*. That book has been used to train thousands of preachers. This godly man was so committed to teaching truth that he did it well even with one blind, sickly student. Broadus paid attention to his life and his doctrine.

Years later, when Broadus delivered the last words he ever said in the classroom, he knew his death was approaching. He was completing a course in New Testament and, after reviewing the lesson, he turned to his students, "Young gentlemen," he said, "if this were the last time I should ever be permitted to address you, I would feel amply repaid for consuming the hour and endeavoring to impress upon you these two things: true piety and, like Apollos, to be men mighty in the Scriptures."

The student who recorded it said that Broadus, after a pause, stood for a moment with his piercing eyes fixed upon his students and repeated over and over again, "Mighty in the Scriptures. Mighty in the Scriptures," until the whole class seemed to be lifted through him and into a sacred nearness to the Master. True piety – pay attention to your life. Mighty in the Scriptures – pay attention to your doctrine.

- A reflection by Donald S. Whitney

—

FOR THE
HEARER

—

ON THE EDGE OF THE PEW

Expository Listening

Dan Dumas

I had never heard of a mud room before to moving to Louisville, Ky., in 2007. We moved from Southern California, and in case you're unaware, the weather in Southern California is beautiful, so we never needed anything like a mud room. We just went back and forth from inside to outside and outside to inside without any concern. But you can't do that in the dank and damp seasonal climate that is Louisville, so these mud rooms are necessary. And, believe it or not, they're a pretty practical invention: You can stop there and get rid of all the wet, stinky filth you (or your kids, or your dog, or your neighbor, or anyone else who can take the blame) accumulated before it destroys the inside of your house. Mud rooms can protect your carpet from being ruined, and it can protect husbands from angry wives.

God's Mud Room

Most churches could use something like this. I'm not talking about an actual mud room, but a place where we can stop and strip away the filth that hinders worship and where we can put on clean clothes to engage in transformational worship.

If we're going to extract the most out of corporate worship, we've got to get rid of our soiled garments of the flesh. We've all got things we need to put off and things we need to put on in the mud room. Fortunately, the book of James provides us with the necessary disciplines to do just that.

James 1:19-25 functions like a mud room in that it gives us a place to be warned, cautioned and re oriented as we approach corporate worship. Healthy churches take their corporate worship seriously, and they rightly place the emphasis of their worship on the preaching of God's Word. It was Martin Luther

> Your pastor should not be the only one working hard during the sermon.

who said that "God's Word cannot be without God's people and, conversely, God's people cannot be without God's Word." God's people need the Word, and they need to be ready to hear it. You need to get rid of any and all distractions while simultaneously tilling the soil of your soul to be ready to receive the proclaimed Word.

If you're at a healthy church, you should expect expository preaching every week. It's good and right to have high expectations of the preaching in your church. But you need to be ready to hear it; don't forget there are two sides to that equation. There's expository preaching and then there's expository listening.

Your pastor should not be the only one working hard during the sermon. Everyone in the pews should be actively engaged in hearing the Word. You should adopt the attitude that Samuel encourages in 1 Samuel 3:10: "Speak Lord, for your servant is listening." We can do this by listening to James who, in vintage James style, gives us a worship blueprint with six disciplines to put into practice in our corporate worship. This is how to become an expository listener and doer.

Open Your Ears

The first of these pithy, crisp commands is to open our ears. James just said in 1:18 that people are born again through the Word of God. Romans 10:17 says the same thing: "Faith comes from hearing, and hearing through the word of Christ." The Word brings new life, and new life brings a new lifestyle. It's the Word of God that saves you, and it's the Word of God that sanctifies you. If you don't open your ears you won't be saved, and you won't be sanctified.

Why would James lead with the discipline of listening when it comes to corporate worship? Because this is the A.D. 40s. The original hearers didn't have Paul's letters to the Thessalonians, to Timothy, to Titus or anything else. They didn't have a copy of the New Testament in front of them. When they gathered to worship, they heard the Scriptures read. They had to pay close attention; listening was how they learned and how they survived. They didn't get to go home and grab their Bible and spend Sunday afternoon ransacking it, they just didn't have that kind of personal access. It was imperative that they come ready to hear, ready to receive and ready to be careful listeners.

The same need exists for us today. And notice that this command is addressed to "every person." It's a corporate appeal that everyone both hear and heed. It's the first duty of every member of every congregation to come eager and ready to hear God's Word. When you sit under God's Word you need to be intentional about your listening. The truth is that there are a lot of people sitting in church with no real intention to listen well and put the sermon into action.

In the first century, if you

It's the first duty of every member of every congregation to come eager and ready to hear God's Word.

were a poor listener you would end up spiritually impoverished, and we shouldn't expect it to be any different today. To listen and hear with no intention of doing anything about it is dangerous.

You need a genuine eagerness and readiness to hear. Peter says that "like newborn infants, long for the pure spiritual milk, that by it you may grow up into salvation" (1 Pet 2:2). There should be an insatiable appetite that marks a genuine believer.

So I ask, are you seizing every opportunity to increase your exposure to God's truth? You likely have voluminous access to preaching throughout the year. It's a privilege to hear that much preaching, but it's your responsibility to take advantage of it in your life.

Close Your Mouth

The second principle is to close your mouth. God gives us two ears and one mouth for a reason. There are times when we simply need to be quiet. Be quick to hear and slow to speak. This is countercultural; we live in a time when most people are slow to hear and quick to speak. We love to hear ourselves talk, don't we? As Benjamin Disraeli said, we become "inebriated with the exuberance of our own verbosity."

But James says it's time to stop. As we gather to worship, James calls the congregation to restrain its tongue. The call to shut your mouth is a companion of the first discipline to listen because you can't listen if you're always talking. You won't be a good listener if you're always speaking. Big talkers are rarely good listeners.

If you know anything about the Book of James, you know that the tongue is a major theme. The tongue (that two-ounce member intentionally incarcerated behind a grill of teeth) causes all sorts of problems when we use it without thinking, or when we make rash commitments to appear godly, or use it both to bless and curse. James says it's best to close your mouth. You'll be held accountable to God for every single word that comes out of your mouth (Matt 12:36), so close your mouth and engage in thoughtful responses instead of premature judgments or boasting.

Control Your Temper

The third principle instructs us to develop a long fuse. When the body gathers in corporate worship, forbearance is crucial. It is absolutely critical for church life that we address and control our bitterness and resentment toward one another. Because, according to James, anger and wrath inhibit worship.

So, how do you become slow to anger? By learning self-control. Anger is a controlled response. Maybe you've never thought of it that way before, but how often do you erupt in anger at work? Probably not often. Why? Because you get fired if you do that. But, for some reason, we don't use that sort of control into our home. You likely think most of your anger is righteous, but don't kid yourself: it's not.

When the body gathers together, there has to be a tremendous amount of forbearance and care for one another. We have to cut each other some slack. Lighten up a little bit. Relax. Uncontrolled anger will result in uncontrolled speech.

> Anger inhibits the godly kind of life that God desires and that corporate worship is intended to encourage.

I've been in far too many nasty, angry church meetings. And James hits the nail on the head: this is nothing but carnal zeal, which offends and grieves everyone, including God. Churches go from lighthouse to towering inferno in a single business meeting. As one commenter rightly acknowledged, anger kills listening, and it opens a lot of mouths. When you speak out of anger, you've ceased to be teachable.

You will not receive the Word of God when you're angry. Why is anger such a big deal in the church? Look at verse 20 of James 1: "The anger of man does not produce the righteousness of God." Anger inhibits the godly kind of life that God desires and that corporate worship is intended to encourage. If you think you're worshipping and you're full of anger, you're fooling yourself. Man's anger does not produce the righteousness or worship of God.

Cleanse Your Heart

This fourth discipline of cleansing your heart is a big one: "Therefore put away all filthiness and rampant wickedness." This is how you are to receive God's Word. You've got to "put away" and get rid of some of what's in your heart. In God's mud room we must first put off the filth before we can be clothed in the soul's appropriate garments.

In the West, we usually shower before we get dressed, and our heart must be similarly cleansed if it's going to be receptive. This is simply the New Testament pattern for sanctification. You see it in Colossians 3; you see it in Ephesians 4. You put off lying, you put on truth telling. Put off anger, put on kindness.

It's not enough to do half of the equation, genuine sanctification requires both. There's removal of the sinful attitude or action and replacement with the commensurate righteous act.

God is not satisfied with partial divesting. He demands a comprehensive cleansing. Put aside all filthiness and wickedness: All your filth, all that remains of wickedness, every known vestige, every former semblance of sin is to be put aside. Your life depends on it. Anything that corrupts and reduces your appetite for the Word of God should be set aside.

This doesn't happen overnight, and it's not something you outgrow. You've got to confess continually, repent continually, and keep short accounts continually as a way of life. It should be your pre-worship habit to get your heart ready.

Maybe the first thing you need to repent of is an unwillingness to listen, or being too quick to speak, or too angry. James is clear that we have to cleanse our hearts if we're going to get the most out of the preaching of God's Word.

Mortify Your Pride

The fifth discipline is to mortify your pride. Verse 21 of James 1 commands us to "receive with meekness the implanted word, which is able to save your souls." It doesn't matter what you wear to church, but as Peter says, you better "clothe yourselves … in humility" (1 Pet 5:5). I plead with you to be teachable, not arrogant. James addresses this later in 4:6 when he says that "God opposes the proud, but gives grace to the humble."

We all face obstacles and troublesome people who at different times oppose us, and we're usually, by God's grace, able to deal with it. But you don't want God to oppose you. Pride is the best way to get stiff-armed in your ability to worship and be sanctified. Pride inhibits the necessary hearing of God's Word.

So many people come to church and think they know it all. They've given the New Testament a good once over, maybe they've even chugged through the Old Testament. But the Christian life isn't something you just figure out and then stop working at. It's a continuous process. You've never "arrived." We've got to break up the hard, fallow ground of pride and arrogance so that the seed of God's Word can take root and transform our lives.

You break up the ground by cultivating humility. You show up on Sunday ready and eager to learn and be changed. You're like a calf at a new gate with your feet stomping every week to hear your pastor preach. You're hungry to have the Word of God implanted. This is not native to the human heart, it has to be cultivated, so if you let your pride go unchecked you won't hear the Word of God. Humility is the soul's appropriate garment if you're going to be an effective expository listener.

Move Your Feet

The sixth discipline is to move your feet to action. This is the post-sermon discipline, to "be doers of the word, and not hearers only." The reason James ends his list of imperatives with this is that it's not enough just to come to church and listen well. That's not expository listening. The Bible never decouples hearing from heeding. Belief and behavior are always linked together, they're inseparable.

You may not know this, but your personal application is your pastor's highest joy. The highest joy I have as a pastor is to hear how God's Word is taking root and transforming lives in my congregation. There's nothing sweeter than that. I promise you that if I called your pastors they would agree wholeheartedly that their greatest joy – what keeps them up late at night, what gets them up early in the morning – is to hear how the Word of God is taking root in your life. They live for washing their people with the Word.

Sadly, what happens in most congregations is that members never tell their pastors what God's doing in their lives. You forget to tell them, or worse, you leave after Sunday morning and say "Hey, good sermon." I'm telling you, that means nothing to your pastor.

They've labored all week in the study trying to extract the

> If you let your pride go unchecked you won't hear the Word of God.

Your personal application is your pastor's highest joy.

meaning and application of the Word of God to feed you, and you just say, "Thanks!" You've got to say the meal's good and why.

So from now on, from this day forward, I plead with you never to tell your pastor, "Good sermon." What you've got to do is walk up and tell him what God is doing in your life through his explication of God's Word. You have to say how the Word of God impacted you. That's what brings your pastor the highest joy. If you walk in the truth and tell him about it, it will be like fuel to his fire.

In other words, as an expository listener you should be an aggressive, early adopter of the text at hand. Remember, biblical hearing assumes biblical heeding. When you hear the Word of God in corporate worship, it should grip you and it should change you. It's a dangerous thing to come together and to sit under the Word of God week after week but have no plans to do anything about it, to have no plans to change, no plan to obey. If that's true of you, James says you're at risk of deceiving yourself.

Conclusion

It's dangerous for your soul and unhelpful to everyone else if you make a habit of careless, sloppy listening. You're going to delude yourself into thinking you're okay, and you'll try to live independent of God's Word. Men, you need to lead in taking action with the sermon. Resist being "Mr. Forgetful" and take action. If you do, you will be blessed beyond measure as you are transformed by the perfect law of liberty.

Be attentive to God's Word and to your life. Become an unstoppable, aggressive, serious corporate expository listener. Your pastors want every member to be more like Christ week-by-week. And to do that you need to be eager to hear. This is what James is calling you to become.

Open your ears, close your mouth, control your temper, cleanse your heart, mortify your pride and move your feet to action. This is what expository listening looks like. This is how to listen, hear and apply the Word of God. It will be a challenge, but it's well worth the effort. ◁◈▷

DID NOT OUR HEARTS BURN?

Expository Reading

Robert L. Plummer

God has preserved for us an invaluable gift and resource in the canon of Scripture. In it we have the very words of God, written over many centuries by many men, and all inspired by one divine mind. He could not have given a better gift with more profitable guidance than he has in the Bible. As the hymn writer said, "How firm a foundation, ye saints of the Lord, is laid for your faith in his excellent word!"

As God's people, and especially as those in the 21st century, we have the privilege of reading God's Word in our own language, in many different versions, with innumerable resources at our disposal. This is a rich blessing and a great responsibility, for to whom much is given much will be required (Luke 12:48). We should strive to read the Bible as well as we can and understand its meaning as clearly as possible. It is a joyful task to dig into the Scriptures, and the more you do it the more skilled you will become in interpreting its content.

In what follows, I hope to provide a few practical tips for you to grow in your ability to read and interpret the Bible faithfully. And as you improve as an expository reader of the Bible, I pray that you will know God more intimately, be a more faithful church member and continue to "grow in the grace and knowledge of our Lord and Savior Jesus Christ" (2 Pet 3:18).

> Prayer is the essential starting point for any study of the Bible.

Approach the Bible in Prayer

The first thing to do on the way to expository reading is assume the appropriate posture for an encounter with God's Word. The Scriptures tell us that the human heart is desperately wicked and deceitful (Jer 17:9). Indeed, the basic human response to God's natural revelation (through conscience or nature) is to suppress it in idolatry (Rom 1:18-23). Even God's people, though given a new nature and the Holy Spirit as a guide, must beware of the deceitful inclinations of their remaining sinful nature. As we approach the Bible, we need to realize that sin affects all of our being – our emotions, wills and rational faculties. We can easily deceive ourselves or be deceived by others. We need the Holy Spirit to instruct and guide us. Thus, prayer is the essential starting point for any study of the Bible.

Read the Bible as a Book That Points to Jesus

In a debate with the Jewish religious leaders in Jerusalem, Jesus said, "You search the Scriptures because you think that in them you have eternal life; and

APPROACHING THE BIBLE IN PRAYER

In Psalm 119, King David serves as a good example of honest self-assessment in his approach to the Scripture. Repeatedly, he prays for insight and redirection. Following is a list of sample petitions within the psalm. Slowly praying through selected verses in Psalm 119 is an excellent way to begin a Bible study session.

- Verse 5: "Oh that my ways may be steadfast in keeping your statutes!"

- Verse 10: "With my whole heart I seek you; let me not wander from your commandments!"

- Verse 12: "Blessed are you, O Lord; teach me your statutes!."

- Verses 17-20: "Deal bountifully with your servant, that I may live and keep your word. Open my eyes, that I may behold wondrous things out of your law. I am a sojourner on the earth; hide not your commandments from me! My soul is consumed with longing for your rules at all times."

- Verses 34-37: "Give me understanding, that I may keep your law and observe it with my whole heart. Lead me in the path of your commandments, for I delight in it. Incline my heart to your testimonies, and not to selfish gain! Turn my eyes from looking at worthless things; and give me life in your ways."

it is they that bear witness about me, yet you refuse to come to me that you may have life" (John 5:39-40; cf., Luke 24:25-27). If we study or teach any part of the Bible without reference to Jesus the Savior, we are not faithful interpreters. Of course, not every text points to Jesus in the same way. The Old Testament promises, anticipates and prepares. The New Testament announces the fulfillment in Christ of all of Israel's law, history, prophecies and institutions. Every passage of Scripture must be read as a chapter in a completed book. As we know how the story wraps up (in Christ's life, death and resurrection), we must always be asking how prior chapters lead to that culmination.

> If we study or teach any part of the Bible without reference to Jesus the Savior, we are not faithful interpreters.

Let Scripture Interpret Scripture

The hermeneutical guideline of "Scripture interpreting Scripture" has long been espoused by Christian interpreters, going back at least to Augustine (A.D. 354-430) and Irenaeus (A.D. 130-200). If we believe that all the Bible is inspired by God and thus noncontradictory, passages of Scripture that are less clear should be interpreted with reference to those that are more transparent in meaning.

Another dimension of letting Scripture interpret Scripture means listening to the full panoply of texts that touch upon a subject. For example, if we were to read God's words to Abraham in Genesis 17:10-12, we might conclude that even today all male worshippers of God must be circumcised. Yet, we read in 1 Corinthians 7:19, "For neither circumcision counts for anything nor uncircumcision, but keeping the commandments of God." By understanding the trajectory of Scripture (that OT Law and promises are fulfilled in Christ), we see that circumcision served a preparatory role for the Jewish nation but is no longer required of God's people. The author of Hebrews says that the

Law is only a shadow of the good things that are coming – not the realities themselves (Heb 10:1). Paul can circumcise a coworker as a means of strategic missionary accommodation to unregenerate Jews (Acts 16:3), but when the basis of salvation is at stake, Paul is unbending (Gal 2:3). This brief survey demonstrates how a nuanced understanding of a subject requires the consideration of multiple biblical texts that touch upon it.

Meditate on the Bible

The Bible is not a book for superficial reading. While it is certainly beneficial to read large portions of Scripture in one sitting, no biblical diet is complete without extended rumination on a smaller portion of text. It is instructive that many Christians have found it best to start their prayers with

> No biblical diet is complete without extended rumination on a smaller portion of text.

quiet and sustained reflection on a small portion of Scripture. God himself provides the words for our prayers in the Bible. The Puritan Thomas Manton (1620-1677) wrote, "Meditation is a middle sort of duty between the Word and prayer, and hath respect to both. The Word feedeth meditation, and meditation feedeth prayer ... These duties must always go hand in hand" (*The Complete Works of Thomas Manton*, vol. 17, *Sermons on Several Texts of Scripture*).

Approach the Bible in Faith and Obedience

The Bible is not a philosophy textbook to be debated; it is a revelation from God to be believed and obeyed. As we believe and obey God's Word, we will experience not only joy (Ps 119:72) but also, more importantly, God's blessing, or approval. James writes:

> But be doers of the word, and not hearers only, deceiving yourselves. For if anyone is a hearer of the word and not a doer, he is like a man who looks intently at his natural face in a mirror. For he looks at himself and goes away and at once forgets what he was like. But the one who looks into the perfect law, the law of liberty,

and perseveres, being no hearer who forgets but a doer who acts, he will be blessed in his doing (Jas 1:22-25).

At the same time, we must remember that obedience to God's Word can never be brought about by increased human effort, but is possible only through Christ. As the apostle John writes,

> For this is the love of God, that we keep his commandments. And his commandments are not burdensome. For everyone who has been born of God overcomes the world. And this is the victory that has overcome the world – our faith. Who is it that overcomes the world except the one who believes that Jesus is the Son of God? (1 John 5:3-5).

Reading God's Word coupled with obedience brings glory to God and will make you a more effective Bible reader.

The person who reads Scripture and does not obey it is self-deceived (Jas 1:22). To claim to know God while consistently and consciously disobeying his Word is to demonstrate the falseness of one's claim. The apostle John writes, "Whoever says 'I know him' but does not keep his commandments is a liar, and the truth is not in him" (1 John 2:4). Reading God's Word coupled with obedience brings glory to God and will make you a more effective Bible reader.

Take Note of the Biblical Genre You Are Reading

If your son were to come home from school and claim to have "a ton" of homework, you would not discipline him for lying. You would understand that he is using hyperbole to express his strong emotions. In the same way, we need to approach the Bible as sympathetic readers, respecting the various genres and authorial assumptions that accompany such genres. For example, the genre of proverbs generally assumes exceptions. Proverbs are wise advice, not fail-proof promises. For example, we read in Proverbs 10:4, "A slack hand causes poverty, but the hand of

> We need to approach the Bible as sympathetic readers, respecting the various genres and authorial assumptions that accompany such genres.

the diligent makes rich." All of us can think of examples from our lives that confirm this proverb. At the same time, most of us likely know a few lazy, rich people. Such exceptions do not make the proverb false. Rather, such exceptions confirm the general rule. Proverbs offer wise advice for ordering our lives, but most of them assume exceptions.

The genre of historical narrative also includes a number of authorial assumptions. For example, the biblical authors employ historical narrative to report many events of which they do not necessarily approve. The author of Judges clearly does not think sacrificing one's daughter is a good thing (Judg 11), though he fails to give his opinion on Jephthah's actions in the immediate context. Similarly, many Scriptures teach that drunkenness is wrong, though the apostle John does not feel the need to note its impropriety in John 2:10, where there is a passing reference to inebriation. (A friend of mine once actually appealed to John 2:10 to make a "biblical" case for excessive drinking.) The author of a historical narrative does not always give explicit sanction or condemnation for behavior reported. One must thoughtfully determine what is simply reported and what is intended as normative.

Be Aware of Historical or Cultural Background Issues

The 66 books of the Bible often assume a reader's familiarity with various cultural practices, geographic markers or political figures. Thus, when an untrained reader simply opens up the book of Isaiah and starts reading about nations that no longer exist and obscure political alliances, he or she might simply close the Bible and say, "This is too hard to understand."

As with any historical document, the reader of the Bible will need study aids to delve into the nuances of background issues. Of course, some of the books of the Bible assume little knowledge on the part of the reader and are quite accessible. The Gospel of John, for example, is often distributed as a stand-alone evangelistic tract for this reason.

Depending on one's familiarity with the Scripture, some background issues may be more or less transparent. Do you know what Passover is? Then you shouldn't have trouble with John the Baptist's description of Jesus as the (Passover) lamb (John 1:29). Are you familiar with Israel's 40 years of wandering the wilderness? Then Jesus' 40-day stay in the wilderness, where he was tested but did not sin, takes on added significance (Matt 4.2, Luke 4:2).

As you study the Bible more, you will have less need to consult commentaries or study aids for the answers to basic questions. There are many introductory surveys of the Old and New Testaments, as well as books specifically on backgrounds, which provide a wealth of information to the curious student.

In discussing Bible backgrounds, we also must note two important caveats. First, one can become so enamored with outside historical, cultural, political or archaeological matters that he essentially ends up using the Bible as a springboard for extrabiblical trivia. The study of ancient Near Eastern culture, while fascinating in its own right, is not the purpose of Bible study.

One must always ask: "Did the biblical author really assume that his readers would know this fact?" And, "If he assumed his readers would know this fact, was it important for the meaning that he was trying to convey?" If the answer to both of these questions is "Yes," then the background issue is indeed worthy of consideration. Unfortunately, in attempts to provide something "fresh" to their congregations, too many pastors are readily taken in by far-fetched interpretations based on some speculative background issue. A pastor's time would be better spent meditating prayerfully on the text to discover genuine text-driven applications.

A second error one must avoid in background issues is to neglect them. In order to understand and apply a text faithfully, one often must have some awareness of the author's historical or cultural assumptions. One cannot understand the denunciations in the Minor Prophets, for example, without knowing something of Israel's prior history and relations to surrounding nations. And, while much of this historical background can be garnered directly from other biblical documents, an uninitiated reader will need the help of a more mature reader's summaries. A study Bible, such as *The HCSB Study Bible* or *ESV Study Bible*, provides brief but helpful comments on relevant background issues.

Pay Attention to Context

Any portion of Scripture must be read within the context of the sentence, paragraph, larger discourse unit and entire book. Attempting to understand or apply a particular biblical phrase or verse without reference to the literary context is virtually guaranteed to result in distortion. Unfortunately, in popular Christian literature and preaching, there are many examples of such failure to respect the context of a passage. One of the most painful exhibits of such hermeneutical failure is a preacher who bullies and blusters about the authority and inerrancy of Scripture while practically denying its authority

Attempting to understand or apply a particular biblical phrase or verse without reference to the literary context is virtually guaranteed to result in distortion.

through his sloppy preaching.

It often has been said, "A text without a context is a pretext," meaning that a preacher will be inclined to infuse a text with his own biases if he does not allow the context to direct him to the authorial intent. I have found this true in my own life. When I am given the opportunity to select a text for a sermon, I sometimes already have an idea of what I want to say. But, as I go back to the text and study it within context, prayerfully meditating over it, the direction of my message often shifts. Holding tightly to the text calls me back to the inspired author's meaning. I tell my students to hold onto the biblical text like a rider in a rodeo holds onto a bull. And, I also warn them that the only persons in the rodeo ring not on bulls are clowns.

When preaching the Bible, I want to be able to place my finger on specific words and phrases in the text to justify my exhortations. As a congregation, you should be persuaded by the words of Scripture, not by the rhetorical ability of a preacher. The power of a sermon or Bible lesson lies in its faithfulness to the inspired text.

Read the Bible in Community

We live in an individualistic age. Yet God created us to live and worship and grow spiritually together in community. The author of Hebrews writes that we should not neglect "to meet together, as is the habit of some, but encouraging one another, and all the more as you see the Day drawing near" (Heb 10:25).

Only as we live out our faith in Christ together do we come to

---

ELEVEN PRINCIPLES FOR BECOMING AN EXPOSITORY READER

1. Approach the Bible in prayer;
2. Read the Bible as a book that points to Jesus;
3. Let Scripture interpret Scripture;
4. Meditate on the Bible;
5. Approach the Bible in faith and obedience;
6. Take note of the biblical genre you are reading;
7. Be aware of historical or cultural background issues;
8. Pay attention to context;
9. Read the Bible in community;
10. Read the Bible; and
11. Read and listen to faithful preaching and teaching.

---

understand with depth and clarity what God has done in and through us (Phlm 6). Similarly, we see that God has structured the church as a "body" and that every member of that body does not have the same function (Rom 12:4-5). Some are more gifted as teachers (Rom 12:7). Others are more gifted in showing mercy or serving in some other way (Rom 12:8). While all God's people are called to read and meditate on his Word (Ps 119:9, 105), some are specially gifted in explaining that Word and exhorting others to believe and obey it (Eph 4:11-13).

If we neglect God's grace to us in the gifting of other believers, how impoverished we will be! Reading the Bible with fellow believers helps us to gain insights that we would otherwise miss. Also, our brothers and sisters can guard us from straying into false interpretations and misapplications.

Read the Bible

When I was 13 years old, my mother gave me a photocopy of a hand-written guide for reading the Bible through in a year. Thus began the most important part of my theological education – immersion in Scripture.

In order to understand the Bible, one must read it. And,

It is essential for any faithful interpreter of the Bible to have read the entire Bible and to continue to read through the Bible regularly.

in order to read the individual parts of the Bible in context, one must read the whole. Thus, it is essential for any faithful interpreter of the Bible to have read the entire Bible and to continue to read through the Bible regularly. Can you imagine a teacher of Milton who admitted to having read only "portions" of *Paradise Lost*? How foolish it is for a minister of the gospel to seek faithfulness in expounding God's Word while remaining ignorant of the contents of that revelation.

If you want to start this kind of habit you can start at Genesis 1 and read three or four chapters per day. By the end of the year, you will have finished the

Bible. Another option is to read portions of both the Old and New Testament every day. The famous Scottish preacher Robert Murray M'Cheyne developed a reading plan that takes one through the Old Testament once and New Testament and Psalms twice over the course of a year – reading about four chapters per day.

I am currently following this reading plan, which is found in an introductory section of D.A. Carson's devotional, *For the Love of God: A Daily Companion for Discovering the Riches of God's Word* (Wheaton: Crossway, 1998). This book has a one-page devotional for each day of the year. At the top of each page is a list of Bible chapters to read for that day, according to M'Cheyne's reading plan. Carson, a leading evangelical New Testament scholar, provides insightful reflections on one chapter from the reading plan each day. I appreciate the way he interprets the passages faithfully while showing how the small pieces fit in the overall vista of Scripture, finding ultimate fulfillment in Christ. Over the course of a year or two, the bite-size chunks of biblical theology, slowly digested, could have quite a beneficial effect on the thoughtful reader.

Read and Listen to Faithful Preaching and Teaching

Faithful interpretation is more easily "caught" than "taught." By reading or listening to faithful expositions of Scripture, one's heart and mind are engaged. Just as the person who regularly drinks fine coffee develops a refined taste for the beverage, a person who consumes a regular diet of faithful teaching develops a mind and heart that is able to recognize good interpretation, as well as distortions.

One of the most important questions you need to ask

Faithful interpretation is more easily "caught" than "taught." By reading or listening to faithful expositions of Scripture, one's heart and mind are engaged.

yourself is, "Am I hearing the Bible faithfully preached and taught at my local church?" If you are not, the second question you should ask yourself is, "Why am I a member of a church where God's Word is not being taught correctly?" If you are not experiencing the edifying and sanctifying effects of biblical teaching, you are likely withering and ineffective in your spiritual life (Col 1:28-29; 2 Peter 1:3-8). If you are receiving a regular diet of biblical edification but only from source(s) outside your church, that is a good indication that you need to seek a new church – one where the pastors faithfully shepherd the flock, feeding them from the Word of God (Acts 20:28).

Although a local church that teaches the Bible faithfully is an absolute necessity, one can also grow spiritually from reading or listening to the sermons and Bible teaching of those outside your local church. Free audio sermons are widely available on the Web. Two websites I recommend are www.truthforlife.org (teaching by Alistair Begg) and www.desiringgod.org (teaching by John Piper and others). There are, of course, many other gifted, faithful preachers to whom you can listen.

One also can learn much from reading sermons, commentaries and devotionals by faithful exegetes. Certainly, the Bible is the Book, but God's gifting of his servants demands that we admit the usefulness of others' books as well. One way to discover useful books or resources is to ask a trusted fellow Christian. Maybe there is someone in your church who has demonstrated a mature

> Just as the person who regularly drinks fine coffee develops a refined taste for the beverage, a person who consumes a regular diet of faithful teaching develops a mind and heart that is able to recognize good interpretation.

> There is no more worthy endeavor than to honor God by seeking to know and understand all that he has said.

knowledge of the Scriptures. Why not ask that person, "What good books have you read recently? Do you have any book recommendations?"

Conclusion

My prayer is that these principles will encourage you to immerse yourself in the Scriptures. There is no more worthy endeavor than to honor God by seeking to know and understand all that he has said. As with all good things that God gives us, they are not for our benefit only. In the spiritual life, you are either a stagnant pool or a flowing fountain. If you are learning but not sharing what you are learning, you will be like an algae-covered pond. You might not be in full-time ministry, but when it comes to the Bible, all of God's people are to overflow with the truths they are learning. Even if your conversations about the Bible are only with your children, spouse and neighbors, you should be seeking to share the new insights you are learning about God. As you move forward in sharing the Scriptures, may you and those you teach cry out to God, "How sweet are your words to my taste, sweeter than honey to my mouth" (Ps 119:103)! ⊗⊗⊗

Adapted from *40 Questions About Interpreting the Bible* © Copyright 2010 by Robert L. Plummer. Published by Kregel Publications, Grand Rapids, MI. Used by permission of the publisher. All rights reserved.

WORTHY OF DOUBLE HONOR

Expository Advocating

James M. Hamilton Jr. with Matt Damico

Preaching is a fool's task. Paul says as much when he tells the Corinthians that "the word of the cross is folly to those who are perishing" (1 Cor 1:17). There are a lot of preachers and congregations who agree so strongly with that diagnosis that they've deemed it necessary to modify the way preaching is done in their church. They've gotten rid of the traditional sermon, which is viewed by some as archaic and abusive, in favor of dialogue and conversation.

Paul was telling the truth when he said that preaching the gospel is folly, but he also says, "God chose what is foolish in the world to shame the wise" (1 Cor 1:27). A commitment to expository preaching takes a firm belief in the power of God's Word and a humble recognition that the God-appointed means of preaching is better than whatever impressive or efficient model we might devise. God will build his church through expository preaching, and it takes a committed fool to believe it and do it. This means there will be times when your pastor feels deeply the reality that he is engaging in a fool's task and will cry out with Paul, "Who is sufficient for these things" (2 Cor 2:16)?

If your preacher is a committed fool, he will need encouragement. That might not seem obvious, but the reality is that the pastorate can be a discouraging place. Not only does the very idea of preaching look foolish in the world's eyes (and occasionally in those of the congregation), but discouragement seems to come from every direction even as he tries to serve the Lord and love his people. Maybe his own sin is overwhelming him and hurting those around him. Maybe there's tension at home. Maybe he can't make ends meet financially.

If you're a member at a church and you're regularly hearing the Bible exposited, you have much for which to be thankful.

Maybe he's feeling inadequate after listening to a John Piper sermon. Maybe a member made a snide comment after a sermon that he can't shake. Maybe it seems like no one follows along as he preaches. Whatever it is, these things take a toll.

That's where you, the church member, come in. If you're a member at a church and you're regularly hearing the Bible exposited, you have much for which to be thankful. If your preacher is diligent to preach the whole counsel of God, to let the content and structure of the text dictate that of his sermon and to apply the Bible to your life so that you're walking in the truth, you are blessed.

Paul says that those who labor faithfully in preaching and teaching are worthy of "double honor" (1 Tim 5:17) and are to be respected and esteemed highly in love (1 Thess 5:12-13). That honor, respect and high estimation is to come from the church members. Hopefully you actually want to encourage your pastor, but you should also see that the Bible exhorts you to do so.

When I use the word "encourage," I don't mean that you should merely say nice things to your pastor to flatter him and make him feel better. I mean you should consider "how to stir up one another to love and good works" (Heb 10:24). As Kevin DeYoung says, encouragement "is not about commending nice people to make them feel good but about commending the work of the gospel in others to the glory of God." Your pastor doesn't need flattery, but he does need genuine, biblical encouragement that helps him keep his hands to the plow as he works to cut a straight path in his ministry. If you're not sure how to do that, then here are some practical ideas for encouraging your pastor.

Pray

"Brothers, pray for us" (1 Thess 5:25). That was the apostle Paul who said that. If the apostle Paul

Pastors are ordinary men, but they hold an extraordinary office.

needed prayer, your pastor does, too. Pastors are ordinary men, but they hold an extraordinary office. The New Testament places unique responsibility on pastors to shepherd God's people by teaching, preaching, counseling, leading and serving. This responsibility carries serious ramifications: pastors will face a stricter judgment (Jas 3:1) and will give account before God for the souls with which they've been entrusted (Heb 13:17). This is not an office to be entered into lightly.

The New Testament is not the only source of pressure that pastors experience, however. Our culture, with all of its resistance to authority and cynicism toward the Bible, eagerly anticipates the next report of a pastor falling into sin. This happens with sickening frequency, and with it comes yet more disrepute on the bride of Christ.

With all of this, it should be clear that one of the most loving

---

EIGHT WAYS TO USE
SCRIPTURE TO PRAY FOR YOUR PASTOR
1 THESS 5:25

Pray that he would conduct himself wisely in a life of obedience that remains above reproach (1 Tim 3:2);

Pray that he would love and be faithful to his wife (Eph 5:25-33);

Pray that he would raise his children in the fear and admonition of the Lord (Eph 6:4);

Pray that he would love the Lord with all his heart, soul, mind and strength (Mk 12:30);

Pray that he would faithfully shepherd the flock of God (1 Pet 5:1-3);

Pray that he would flee temptation (1 Thess 4:3-8);

Pray that he would be a man of unceasing prayer (Eph 6:18); and

Pray that he would bind himself to the Scriptures and commit himself to expounding the Word of God rather than his own opinions (2 Tim 4:1-4).

---

and faithful things you can do as a church member is to pray for your pastor. Pray for him as you prepare for church, pray for him with your family, with other church members or ask him if you can pray for him in person.

There are a host of ways you can pray for your pastor: Pray that he would conduct himself wisely in a life of obedience that remains above reproach (1 Tim 3:2); pray that he would love and be faithful to his wife (Eph 5:25-33); pray that he would raise his children in the fear and admonition of the Lord (Eph 6:4); pray that he would love the Lord with all his heart, soul, mind and strength (Mk 12:30); pray that he would faithfully shepherd the flock of God (1 Pet 5:1-3); pray that he would flee temptation (1 Thess 4:3-8); pray that he would be a man of unceasing prayer (Eph 6:18) and pray that he would bind himself to the Scriptures and commit himself to expounding the Word of God rather than his own opinions (2 Tim 4:1-4). This list is by no means exhaustive, but there is no better place to start than by praying God's own words for your pastor.

Prepare

The last thing a pastor or preacher wants to think is that he is the

Satan will use anything he can to keep God's people from fully engaging in worship.

only one prepared for Sunday morning. That doesn't mean you need to write your own sermon during the week, but you might be surprised how much more you get out of your Sunday mornings by simply being more prepared.

The truth is that Sunday morning begins on Saturday night. There are a number of extremely practical ways to be prepared for worship, all for the purpose of removing potential distractions and obstacles. On the physical side, consider laying out and ironing clothes for yourself and your family the night prior, be sure that the car is gassed up, pack any bags with Bibles and diapers and whatever else you bring as a family, make sure the alarms are set, get plenty of rest the night before, have breakfast planned and ready to go for the morning. All of these things, as simple as they may seem, will eliminate potential distractions on Sunday morning.

You don't need to make a rule out of these things; we all know that life happens, but they are helpful means of removing potential stumbling blocks. You might think they're unimportant, but Satan will use anything he can to keep God's people from fully engaging in worship.

There are, of course, ways to be spiritually prepared as well. Take some time to pray alone or as a family, confess sins to one another that need to be confessed, sing songs of praise together at dinner on Saturday and read Scripture together. In fact, there's a way you can read Scripture in preparation for worship that just may be the most significant way

---

HOW TO PREPARE FOR WORSHIP

Physically
1. Lay out and iron clothes for yourself and your family on Saturday night;
2. Be sure that the car is gassed up;
3. Pack any bags with Bibles and diapers and whatever else you bring as a family;
4. Make sure the alarms are set;
5. Get plenty of rest the night before; and
6. Have breakfast planned and ready to go for the morning.

Spiritually
7. Pray alone and as a family;
8. Confess sins to one another;
9. Sing songs of praise together at dinner on Saturday;
10. Read Scripture together; and
11. Read the sermon text.

---

to prepare for worship. This isn't something I thought up myself, rather, the Lord's dear people at Kenwood Baptist Church in Louisville, Ky., where I pastor, have encouraged me in this way and I'm offering it so the blessing can be multiplied.

Here's what you do: find out what text is going to be preached, and read the passage before you come to church. It's simple and it's good for you and it will encourage your pastor.

There are different ways to do it. Maybe you could read the sermon text at the breakfast table before you go to church, or maybe sometime on Saturday will work better for you. There are a number of ways your pastor will be encouraged by this: he'll be encouraged by your asking what he'll preach, and your telling him that you're asking because you like to read the passage in preparation for worship. He'll be encouraged when you ask him after church how to understand something you saw in the text that he didn't have time to address in the sermon. He'll be encouraged to see the Spirit of God drawing you to the Word of God – getting to hear that you're reading the Bible will be like the farmer seeing fruit on those vines he's been tending – what a joy to know that the people you serve are reading the Bible! He'll be encouraged if you tell him you had trouble seeing the relevance of the passage, or understanding it, and then were helped by his sermon. He'll be encouraged to hear that his sermon made you want to go back and read the passage more carefully, or to meditate on it more. He'll be encouraged when you tell him that his preaching has helped you to become a better Bible reader.

Most importantly, he'll be encouraged to see you apply the sermon by walking in the truth. One elder wrote about the people in the churches he served: "I have no greater joy than to hear that my children are walking in the truth" (3 John 1:4). In fact, he said that kind of thing repeatedly (cf., 1 John 1:4;

Nothing will encourage your pastor like giving him the joy of seeing you walk in the truth.

A SAMPLE OF WAYS TO ENGAGE IN MINISTRY

1. Encourage other members;
2. Outdo others in showing honor;
3. Love others, especially those on the fringes;
4. Do evangelism;
5. Visit and encourage the elderly and homebound;
6. Meet in accountability with other members to encourage godliness;
7. Give financially;
8. Do missions;
9. Mentor someone younger in the faith;
10. Clean the church building;
11. Serve in children's ministry;
12. Drive people to church who need rides; and
13. Teach Sunday school.

2 John 1:4; 3 John 1:3-4). Nothing will encourage your pastor like giving him the joy of seeing you walk in the truth. Read the sermon text before church on Sunday and be conformed to the image of Christ from one degree of glory to another.

Participate

In Ephesians 4, Paul tells us that God gave to the church, among other things, "shepherds and teachers." Shepherds and teachers is simply another way of saying "pastors." Paul is saying that your pastor is actually a gift from God. He's still a sinner, but he's a gift. Notice that Paul tells us that God's purpose in giving these pastors is "to equip the saints for the work of ministry, for building up the body of Christ" (Eph 4:11-13).

Does your church have the mentality that the pastor is there to be the professional and do the ministry and you are there simply to receive it week after week? That's not how God arranged it. The pastor is indeed there to do ministry, but much of his ministry consists of equipping and building up God's people to do ministry. As we noted above, nothing will give your pastor more joy than seeing you walk in the truth, and part of what that means is that you engage your heart and hands in the task of ministry. This isn't simply to help your pastor do his job, it's for the good of your soul and the health of the church.

Most of the New Testament's epistles were written as letters to specific churches, where the many commands and exhortations to care for, comfort, encourage, forgive, honor, love and serve "one another" were not just abstract instructions. When people heard those letters read for the first time, they knew the actual people who were to receive their care, comfort, encouragement, forgiveness, honor, love and service.

They had pastors to preach and teach Scripture, to pray and to watch over their souls. But much of the horizontal person-to-person ministry was done by the church members. A church that lives like this is rare, precious. Too many view their pastors as professionals (and some pastors view themselves this way) and church members view themselves as consumers who come to church to get what they can from the church's "products." This might seem to be the more efficient way to do ministry, but this is not the way a body functions, and it isn't the way church should be.

> Does your church have the mentality that the pastor is there to be the professional and do the ministry and you are there simply to receive it week after week? That's not how God arranged it.

The task of a New Testament church is to be faithful, not merely efficient.

The New Testament's vision of church ministry is rare, but it's been given to us by God, and the task of a New Testament church is to be faithful, not merely efficient.

Rather than improving the real fruitfulness of a church, this sort of arrangement actually augments the strain on and discouragement of the pastor. There are few things as encouraging to a pastor as seeing his people living as Christians and doing ministry.

There are all sorts of ways to participate in your church's ministry. You could encourage other members, outdo others in showing honor, love others – especially those on the fringes, do evangelism, visit and encourage the elderly and homebound, meet in accountability with other members to encourage godliness, give financially, do missions, mentor someone younger in the faith, clean the church building, serve in children's ministry, drive people to church who need rides, teach Sunday school and all sorts of other things.

Your pastor will be energized to keep at the task of equipping and building up the saints as he sees the members of the church acting like Christians, like people who love and follow Jesus.

Conclusion

This is just the beginning. Praying, preparing and participating are just three ways you can encourage your pastor, and there are many more.

As you support and advocate for your pastor like this, you will indeed be showing him the double honor of which Paul speaks, you'll be esteeming him highly and you will be honoring God. ∞

Resources

Further Reading

On the Preparation and Delivery of Sermons, John A. Broadus

He Is Not Silent: Preaching in a Postmodern World, R. Albert Mohler Jr.

Between Two Worlds: The Challenge of Preaching Today, John Stott

Rediscovering Expository Preaching, John MacArthur

The Supremacy of God in Preaching, John Piper

Preaching and Preachers, D. Martyn Lloyd-Jones

Feed My Sheep: A Passionate Plea for Preaching, Don Kistler, ed.

Nine Marks of a Healthy Church, Mark Dever

What Is a Healthy Church Member, Thabiti M. Anyabwile

THE CENTER FOR CHRISTIAN PREACHING
The Center for Christian Preaching is an international center that is unapologetically committed to modeling and promoting expository preaching.

From Southern Seminary

Also in the Guide Book Series from SBTS Press, available at press.sbts.edu

A Guide to Biblical Manhood (SBTS Press, 2011 $5.99), Randy Stinson and Dan Dumas

A Guide to Adoption and Orphan Care (SBTS Press, 2012 $5.99), Russell D. Moore, Editor

PUBLICATIONS FROM SOUTHERN SEMINARY
Southern Seminary Magazine

Towers: A News Publication of The Southern Baptist Theological Seminary

The Southern Baptist Journal of Theology

The Journal of Discipleship and Family Ministry

The Southern Baptist Journal of Missions and Evangelism

CONNECT WITH SOUTHERN SEMINARY ONLINE
News.sbts.edu
Facebook.com/TheSBTS
Twitter.com/SBTS

For more information about Southern Seminary, visit sbts.edu; for information about Boyce College, visit boycecollege.com

Contributors

Editor

DAN DUMAS is a church planter and teaching pastor at Eastside Community Church in Louisville, Ky. He is passionate about leadership, expository preaching, biblical manhood and being a transformational ministry architect. He is the co-author of *A Guide to Biblical Manhood*. Dumas became senior vice president at Southern Seminary in October 2007. He came to Louisville from Grace Community Church in Sun Valley, Calif., where he served as elder, executive pastor, pastor of assimilation, director of conferences and pastor of the Cornerstone Fellowship Group. Prior to joining the staff at Grace, Dan logged extensive ministry hours at many local churches. He is married to Jane and has two children.

Contributors

JAMES M. HAMILTON JR. is associate professor of biblical theology at Southern Seminary and preaching pastor at Kenwood Baptist Church in Louisville, Ky. He is the author of *Revelation: The Spirit Speaks to the Churches*, *God's Glory in Salvation through Judgment: A Biblical Theology* and *God's Indwelling Presence: The Ministry of the Holy Spirit in the Old and New Testaments*. He is married to Jill and has four children.

R. ALBERT MOHLER JR. is the ninth president of The Southern Baptist Theological Seminary. He also serves as professor of Christian theology at the seminary. Mohler is the author of *He is Not Silent*, *Culture Shift*, *Desire and Deceit* and several other books. Mohler hosts two podcasts: "The Briefing," and "Thinking in Public." He also writes a popular blog with regular commentary on moral, cultural and theological issues, all of which can be accessed at www.AlbertMohler.com. Mohler is an ordained minister, and has served as pastor and staff minister of several Southern Baptist churches. He is married to Mary and has two children.

RUSSELL D. MOORE is senior vice president for academic administration and dean of the School of Theology at The Southern Baptist Theological Seminary in Louisville, Ky. Moore writes and speaks frequently on topics ranging from the kingdom of God to the mission of adoption to a theology of country music. He is a senior editor of *Touchstone: A Journal of Mere Christianity* and also blogs regularly at Moore to the Point: russellmoore.com. He is the author of such books as *Tempted and Tried: Temptation and the Triumph of Christ, Adopted for Life: The Priority of Adoption for Christian Families and Churches* and *The Kingdom of Christ: The New Evangelical Perspective*. Prior to entering the ministry, he was an aide to U.S. Congressman Gene Taylor. He and his wife Maria have five sons.

ROBERT L. PLUMMER is associate professor of New Testament interpretation at The Southern Baptist Theological Seminary in Louisville, Ky. Plummer is the author of *40 Questions About Interpreting the Bible* (Kregel, 2010, from which the material in this book was adapted), *Paul's Understanding of the Church's Mission, Did the Apostle Paul Expect the Early Christian Communities to Evangelize?* and many other articles and essays. Plummer is an elder at Sojourn Community Church in Louisville. He has served on mission assignments in China, Malaysia, Ghana, Israel, Turkey and Trinidad. He and his wife Chandi have three daughters.

DONALD S. WHITNEY is associate professor of biblical spirituality and senior associate dean at The Southern Baptist Theological Seminary in Louisville, Ky. He is the founder and president of The Center for Biblical Spirituality. Prior to his ministry as a seminary professor, Whitney was pastor of Glenfield Baptist Church in Glen Ellyn, Ill. for almost 15 years. Altogether, he has served local churches in pastoral ministry for 24 years. He is the author of *Spiritual Disciplines for the Christian Life*. He is married to Caffy and has one daughter.

Production

PROJECT EDITOR:
MATT DAMICO is a staff writer for Southern Seminary. He earned a bachelor of arts in English from the University of Minnesota in 2008 before moving to Louisville, Ky. He graduated from Southern with a master of divinity in 2012, and currently serves as minister of worship at Kenwood Baptist Church in Louisville. He is married to the wonderful Anna.

DESIGNER:
ANDREA STEMBER joined Southern Seminary's creative team in 2011 after working four years in the Chicago, Ill., graphic design scene. Though she loves the city, Andrea was born and raised in the state of Iowa, where she earned her bachelor of fine arts degree in graphic design from Iowa State University. She is married to Daniel.

A Guide to Expository Ministry illustrations produced by Ray Rieck, whose work can be seen at www.rayrieck.com

Made in the USA
San Bernardino, CA
06 March 2016